McGraw-Hill's

CAREERS FOR

SCIENTIFIC TYPES

& Others with Inquiring Minds

Careers for You Series

McGraw-Hill's

CAREERS FOR

SCIENTIFIC TYPES

& Others with Inquiring Minds

Jan Goldberg

SECOND EDITION

New York Chicago San Francisco Lisbon London Madrid Mexico City
Milan New Delhi San Juan Seoul Singapore Sydney Toronto

The **McGraw·Hill** Companies

Library of Congress Cataloging-in-Publication Data

Goldberg, Jan.
  Careers for scientific types & others with inquiring minds / Jan Goldberg —
2nd ed.
    p.   cm. — (McGraw-Hill careers for you series)
    ISBN 0-07-147618-0 (alk. paper)
    1. Science—Vocational guidance.   2. Technology—Vocational guidance.
  I. Title.   II. Title: Careers for scientific types and others with inquiring minds.

Q147.G64 2007
502.3—dc22   2006028897

1 2 3 4 5 6 7 8 9 10 11 12 13 14 15   DOC/DOC   0 9 8 7

ISBN-13: 978-0-07-147618-8
ISBN-10:   0-07-147618-0

McGraw-Hill books are available at special quantity discounts to use as premiums and
sales promotions, or for use in corporate training programs. For more information,
please write to the Director of Special Sales, Professional Publishing, McGraw-Hill,
Two Penn Plaza, New York, NY 10121-2298. Or contact your local bookstore.

This book is printed on acid-free paper.

To the memory of my beloved parents,
Sam and Sylvia Lefkovitz, and the
memory of a dear uncle, Bernard Lefko

Contents

Acknowledgments

The author gratefully acknowledges the following individuals for their contributions:

- The numerous professionals who graciously agreed to be profiled in this book
- My dear husband, Larry, for his inspiration and vision
- My children—Sherri, Deborah, and Bruce—for their encouragement and love
- Family and close friends—Adrienne, Marty, Mindi, Cary, Michele, Paul, Michele, Alison, Steve, Marci, Steve, Brian, Steven, Jesse, Collin, Andrew, Bertha, and Aunt Helen—for their kindness and support
- Diana Catlin for her insights and input

The editors would like to thank Josephine Scanlon for her work on this revision.

CHAPTER ONE

Is the Scientific Path Right for You?

Science is built up of facts, as a house is built of stones;
but an accumulation of facts is no more a science
than a heap of stones is a house.
—Henri Poincaré

D id you know that for most of history, people thought that blood didn't move in the body at all? Enter William Harvey, the man who is credited with discovering that blood circulates. In a series of classic experiments, Harvey established the role of the heart and a modern picture of the circulatory system. As a typical experiment, he put a tourniquet on a subject's arm, and when the veins popped, pressed on them to see which direction was "downstream." This is how he discovered that blood in the veins always flows toward the heart.

In 1955 at the University of Chicago, Harold Urey and Stanley Miller performed an experiment that demonstrated how the first step in chemical evolution may have taken place. They combined methane, hydrogen, ammonia, and carbon dioxide—the materials believed to be the components of the earth's early atmosphere—and subjected the mixture to electrical sparks (thus simulating the effects of lightning). In a matter of hours they noticed that the constituents of early earth were forming molecules known as amino acids, which are the basic building blocks of proteins. In other words, Miller and Urey, starting with nonliving materials, had produced the simplest materials that make up the living cell.

In 1919, Arthur (later Sir Arthur) Eddington made what most people regard as the most dramatic and best-known confirmation of the theory of relativity. Traveling to the coast of Africa to observe a solar eclipse, he noted that the position of stars near the edge of the sun appeared to be shifted during the eclipse, a shift that could only occur if light from the stars were bent as it went around the sun.

The regularly spaced signals from a pulsar (cosmic source of pulses of radiation) look a lot like an attempt at communication from extraterrestrials. In fact, when astronomers in England first detected them in the late 1960s, they were referred to as LGM (little green men) signals by people in the observatory.

If you find these facts fascinating, perhaps you are a scientific type at heart. What kind of person do you need to be to most successfully enter the world of science? Take the following quiz, answering yes or no to each question. You may discover that you are, indeed, a scientific type and that one of the careers profiled within this book might be just perfect for you!

The Scientific Path—Do You Have What It Takes?

1. Do you enjoy working on long-term projects?
2. Are you a self-starter who can work alone?
3. Can you deal with "failures"—situations that don't produce the predicted result—effectively?
4. Do you have a long attention span?
5. Can you work effectively as part of a team?
6. Do you enjoy working independently on a day-to-day basis?

7. Is the idea of exploring the unknown interesting to you?
8. Do you have a strong interest in the world of science?
9. Are your math skills adequate?
10. Are you willing to earn at least a bachelor's degree?
11. Do you have strong skills in logic and problem solving?
12. Do you wish to be a part of something that could contribute to the betterment of humanity?

Scientific types and those with inquiring minds have made incredible contributions to society ever since the beginnings of recorded history. Are you interested in joining that group? This book outlines a wide variety of careers that are options for you. The list is certainly not all-inclusive, but it does provide a variety of possibilities.

Perhaps someday your name will be listed along with other scientific types mentioned in the pages of this book!

CHAPTER TWO

Careers in the Biological and Medical Sciences

The essence of science: Ask an impertinent question, and you are on the way to a pertinent answer.
—Jacob Bronowski

Inquiring minds helped the following scientific types to find a place in the history books by distinguishing themselves with notable achievements: Scotsman Sir Alexander Fleming discovered penicillin in 1928; Frenchman Louis Pasteur developed germ theory in 1861; bacteria was first observed by Dutchman Antoni van Leeuwenhoek in 1683; and American Jonas Salk developed the polio vaccine in 1952.

The importance of the biological and medical sciences cannot be underestimated. If you might consider this your calling, here's what you need to know.

Biological and Medical Scientists

Biological and medical scientists are devoted to studying living organisms and their relationships to their environments. Most of these professionals specialize in some area of biology, such as zoology (the study of animals) or microbiology (the study of microscopic organisms).

Research and development is an important part of most medical and biological scientists' work. Some conduct basic research in an effort to increase our knowledge of living organisms. Others work in applied research, using knowledge provided by basic research to develop new medicines, increase crop yields, and improve the environment. Researchers usually work in laboratories using electron microscopes, computers, thermal cyclers, and a wide variety of other equipment; some may conduct experiments on laboratory animals or greenhouse plants. A number of biological scientists perform a substantial amount of research outside of laboratories. For example, a botanist may do research in tropical rain forests to see what plants grow there, or an ecologist may study how a forest area recovers after a fire.

Some biological and medical scientists pursue careers in management or administration. Possible settings might include directing activities at zoos or botanical gardens or managing a research facility. Biological scientists may also work as consultants to business firms or to government, while others test and inspect foods, drugs, and other products or write for technical publications. Others work in sales and service jobs for companies that manufacture chemicals or other technical products.

Advances at the genetic and molecular levels of biological science continue to spur the field of biotechnology forward. Medical and biological scientists use this knowledge to manipulate the genetic material of animals or plants, attempting to make organisms more productive or disease resistant. The first application of this technology occurred in the medical and pharmaceutical areas. Many substances not previously available in large quantities are now produced by biotechnological means—some may be useful in treating cancer and other diseases. Advances in biotechnology have opened up research opportunities in almost all areas of biology, including commercial applications in agriculture and the food and chemical industries.

Today, many biological scientists are involved in biotechnology. Those who work on the Human Genome Project isolate genes and determine their function, work that continues to lead to the discovery of the genes associated with specific diseases and inherited traits, such as obesity or certain types of cancer. These advances have created research opportunities in almost all areas of biology, with commercial applications in the food industry, agriculture, and environmental remediation, and in other emerging areas such as DNA fingerprinting.

Most biological scientists who come under the broad category of biologist are further classified by the types of organisms they study or by the specific activities they perform, although recent advances in the understanding of basic life processes at both the molecular and cellular levels have blurred some of these traditional classifications.

Aquatic Biologists

Aquatic biologists study plants and animals that live in water. Marine biologists study saltwater organisms, and limnologists study freshwater organisms. Marine biologists are sometimes incorrectly called oceanographers—oceanography is the study of the physical characteristics of oceans and the ocean floor.

Biochemists

Biochemists study the chemical composition of living things. They try to understand the complex chemical combinations and reactions involved in metabolism, reproduction, growth, and heredity. Much of biotechnology, which involves understanding the complex chemistry of life, is done by biochemists and molecular biologists.

Botanists

Botanists study plants and their environments. Some study all aspects of plant life; others specialize in areas such as identification and classification of plants, the structure and function of plant parts, the biochemistry of plant processes, the causes and cures of plant diseases, and the geological ancestry of plants.

Microbiologists

Microbiologists investigate the growth and characteristics of microscopic organisms such as bacteria, algae, or fungi. Medical microbiologists study the relationship between organisms and disease or the effect of antibiotics on microorganisms. Others may specialize in environmental, food, agricultural, or industrial microbiology; virology (the study of viruses); or immunology (the study of mechanisms that fight infections). Many use biotechnology as they advance knowledge of cell reproduction and human disease.

Physiologists

Physiologists study life functions of plants and animals under normal and abnormal conditions, both in the whole organism and at the cellular or molecular level. They may specialize in functions such as growth, reproduction, photosynthesis, respiration, or movement, or in the physiology of a certain area or system of the organism.

Zoologists

Zoologists study animals—their origins, behaviors, diseases, and life processes. Some experiment with live animals in controlled or natural surroundings, while others dissect dead animals to learn more about that species. Zoologists are usually identified by the animal group they study—for example, ornithologists (birds), mammalogists (mammals), herpetologists (reptiles and amphibians), or ichthyologists (fish).

Ecologists

Ecologists study relationships, both those among organisms and those between organisms and their environments. They also focus on the effects of influences such as population size, pollutants, rainfall, temperature, and altitude.

Medical Scientists

Biological scientists who conduct biomedical research are usually called medical scientists. Those working in basic research study the functioning of normal biological systems in order to discover the causes and treatment of diseases and other health problems. They often try to identify the kinds of changes in a cell, chromosome, or gene that signal the development of medical problems, such as different types of cancer. After identifying structures or changes in organisms that provide clues to health problems, medical scientists may then work on treatments.

For example, a medical scientist involved in cancer research might try to formulate a combination of drugs that will lessen the effects of the disease. Those with medical degrees might then administer the drugs to patients in clinical trials, monitor patient reactions, and observe the results. (Those who don't have medical degrees usually collaborate with the medical doctor who deals directly with patients.) The medical scientist might then return to the laboratory to examine the results and, if necessary, adjust the dosage levels to reduce negative side effects or to try to induce even better results. In addition to using basic research to develop treatments for health problems, they attempt to discover ways to prevent health problems from developing, such as affirming the link between smoking and increased risk of lung cancer, or alcoholism and liver disease.

Education and Training

If you hope to conduct independent research, work in an administrative position, or teach at the college level, a doctoral degree is your educational requirement. A master's degree is sufficient for some jobs in applied research and for jobs in management, inspection, sales, and service. A bachelor's degree is adequate for some nonresearch jobs.

Some graduates with bachelor's degrees start as biological scientists in testing and inspection or get jobs related to biological science, such as technical sales or service representatives. Occasionally, a bachelor's degree enables you to work in a laboratory environment on your own projects or to work as a research assistant. Other options include working as a biological technician, medical laboratory technologist, or, with courses in education, high school biology teacher. A bachelor's degree in biology also provides a good foundation for entering medical, dental, veterinary, or other health profession schools.

Most colleges and universities offer bachelor's degrees in biological science, and many offer advanced degrees. Curricula for advanced degrees often emphasize a subfield, such as microbiology or botany, and include classroom and fieldwork, laboratory research, and a thesis or dissertation. After earning a doctoral degree (Ph.D.) in biological science, you will be qualified for temporary postdoctoral research positions that provide specialized research experience.

To succeed as a biological scientist, you need to be capable of working effectively on your own or as part of a team. In addition, you must be able to communicate clearly and concisely, both orally and in writing. If you plan to work in private industry and aspire to management or administrative positions, you should also possess good business skills and be familiar with regulatory issues and marketing and management techniques. You need physical stamina if your work includes conducting field research in remote areas.

If medical science is your goal, then a Ph.D. in a biological science is your minimum education requirement because the work is almost entirely research oriented. Earning this advanced degree qualifies you to perform research on basic life processes or on particular medical problems or diseases and to analyze and interpret the results of experiments on patients. You need a medical degree (M.D.) to administer drug or gene therapy to human patients or to otherwise interact medically with patients (drawing blood, excising tissue, or performing other invasive procedures). Many medical scientists earn both Ph.D. and M.D. degrees; a number of schools offer combined M.D./Ph.D. programs.

In addition to your formal education, you'll also be expected to spend several years in a postdoctoral position before being offered a permanent job. Postdoctoral work provides valuable laboratory experience, including a background in specific processes and techniques (such as gene splicing) that are later transferable to other research projects. In some institutions, postdoctoral positions can lead to permanent positions.

Job Outlook

While employment of biological and medical scientists is expected to increase up to 17 percent through 2014, as biotechnological research and development continues to drive job growth, candidates with doctorates should be prepared to face strong competition for basic research positions. Although recent budget increases at the National Institutes of Health have led to large increases in federal basic research and development expenditures, this increase is expected to slow significantly over the next several years, resulting in a highly competitive environment for winning and renewing research grants. In addition, if the number of advanced degrees awarded continues to grow, applicants for research grants are likely to face even more competition. Currently, about one in three grant proposals are approved for long-term research projects. Applied research positions in private industry may become more difficult to obtain if increasing numbers of scientists seek jobs in private industry because of the competitive job market for independent research positions in universities and for college and university faculty.

Opportunities are expected to be better for those with bachelor's or master's degrees in biological science, because the number of science-related jobs in sales, marketing, and research management for which they are qualified is expected to exceed the number of independent research positions. Those without doctorates also may fill positions as science or engineering technicians or as medical health technologists and technicians; some may become high school biology teachers.

Biological scientists enjoyed very rapid gains in employment between the mid-1980s and mid-1990s, reflecting, in part, increased staffing requirements in new biotechnology companies. Employment growth should slow somewhat, along with a slowdown in the number of new biotechnology firms; some existing firms will merge or be absorbed by larger biotechnology or pharmaceutical firms. However, much of the basic biological research done in recent years has resulted in new knowledge, including the isolation and identification of genes. Biological scientists will be needed to take this knowledge to the next stage so that gene therapies can be developed to treat diseases.

Even pharmaceutical and other firms not solely engaged in biotechnology use biotechnology techniques extensively, spurring employment increases for biological scientists. For example, biological scientists are continuing to help farmers increase crop yields by pinpointing genes that can help crops such as wheat grow worldwide in areas that currently are hostile to the crop. Expected expansion of research related to health issues such as AIDS, cancer, and Alzheimer's disease also should create more jobs for these scientists. In addition, efforts to discover new and improved ways to clean up and preserve the environment should continue to add to job growth. More biological scientists will be needed to determine the environmental impact of industry and government actions and to prevent or correct environmental problems such as the negative effects of pesticide use. Some biological scientists will find opportunities in environmental regulatory agencies; others will use their expertise to advise lawmakers on legislation to save environmentally sensitive areas. There will continue to be demand for those specializing in botany, zoology, and marine biology, but opportunities will be limited because of the small size of these fields. New industrial applications of biotechnology, such as changing how companies make ethanol for transportation fuel, will also be a source of employment.

Marine biology is a very small specialty, despite its attractiveness as a career, and those who would like to enter this field far outnumber the very few openings that occur each year for the type of glamorous research jobs that many would like to obtain. Almost all marine biologists who work in basic research have a doctorate.

Biological scientists are less likely to lose their jobs during recessions than are those in many other occupations because many are employed on long-term research projects. However, an economic downturn could influence the amount of money allocated to new research and development efforts, particularly in areas of risky or innovative research. An economic downturn also could limit the possibility of extension or renewal of existing projects.

Salaries

According to the National Association of Colleges and Employers, beginning salary offers in July 2005 averaged $31,258 a year for bachelor's degree recipients in biological and life sciences.

Median annual earnings of biochemists and biophysicists were $68,950 in 2004, with most earning between $49,430 and $88,540. Ten percent earned less than $38,710, and 10 percent earned more than $110,660.

For microbiologists, median annual earnings were $54,840 in 2004; most earned between $41,000 and $74,260. Ten percent earned less than $32,630, and 10 percent earned more than $101,720.

Zoologists and wildlife biologists had median annual earnings of $50,330 in 2004. The majority earned between $39,150 and $63,800, while 10 percent earned less than $31,450, and 10 percent earned more than $81,200.

For biochemists and biophysicists employed in scientific research and development services, the median annual income was $73,900.

In 2005, general biological scientists employed by the federal government in nonsupervisory, supervisory, and managerial positions earned an average salary of $69,908; microbiologists, $80,798; ecologists, $72,021; physiologists, $93,208; geneticists, $85,170; zoologists, $101,601; and botanists, $62,207.

Parade of Professionals

The following professionals work in different areas of research. Read their stories to see whether any of these interesting fields appeals to you.

Amadeo J. Pesce, Ph.D., Toxicology Researcher

Dr. Amadeo Pesce serves as the director of the toxicology laboratory and professor of experimental medicine at the University of Cincinnati Hospital. He has been associated with the University of Cincinnati for the past thirty years. Dr. Pesce earned a B.S. in biology at the Massachusetts Institute of Technology, followed by a Ph.D. in biochemistry from Brandeis University. He served his postdoctoral fellowship at the University of Illinois at Urbana-Champaign and is board certified by the American Board for Clinical Chemistry, which requires five years of experience and successful completion of an examination. Dr. Pesce says that he always knew he was interested in medical research, so his studies were focused on achieving that career goal.

Most of Dr. Pesce's work is conducted as part of a team of researchers. The composition of the team may change, depending on the project, and may include postdoctoral fellows, part-time or full-time technologists, pathologists, mathematicians, psychiatrists, substance abuse counselors, and other health and scientific professionals.

Dr. Pesce and his team usually work on several projects simultaneously. He describes a time when the team was involved in helping with clinical trials in developing methods of measurement for different projects. The goal of one study was to help pace patients by monitoring the effectiveness of the drug AZT, which is used in the treatment of AIDS. The research team developed the technology to measure the concentration of drugs inside a cell and worked very closely with the clinician and the clinical trials that were being conducted.

Another project involved the study of developing agents that help combat substance abuse by reducing the craving and the other aspects that make people want to continue to use drugs. In this situation, the team worked with a group of psychiatrists and substance abuse counselors who provided specimens from the patients for the researchers to monitor.

"In addition to the hours spent in the laboratory, a considerable portion of my time is spent thinking and writing," Dr. Pesce says. "One must think things through and be able to communicate them effectively and efficiently in order for the research to have meaning. And, as I convey to my students, if it's not written down, it was never done."

In his capacity as administrator, Dr. Pesce has other responsibilities in addition to his research. He supervises a postdoctoral fellow and handles personnel and administrative issues. He now keeps fairly regular working hours, but for many years Dr. Pesce worked from 7 A.M. until 10 P.M., five days a week. But that doesn't mean that he took weekends off—the other two days of the week, he worked eight to ten hours.

Dr. Pesce explains the reasons for this intense schedule. "This was not required, but just my own enthusiasm showing, based upon my decision to be one of the four most recognized authorities in the field. So I set on a path of learning all I could and then proceeded to put out a series of books (eighteen) about the field. This required an immense amount of work. I tell everyone that I did this to become rich and famous. (My children always told me to skip the fame!) But as it turns out, all I got was the fame. However, even though I didn't make the money I had hoped for, it has still been very rewarding. Fans as far away as Australia have asked me to sign their copies of my books."

In addition to fame, Dr. Pesce cites other rewards of his challenging career. The first is the accomplishment of developing a theory and finding supporting data. This is particularly satisfying because research projects are funded grants for which investigators must show results by a certain date in order to receive funding for additional projects.

The downside of the job, to Dr. Pesce, is when a paper is rejected by peer reviewers, especially when he knows that his results are correct and the review is not. Despite this, however, he is proud to have done some pioneering work that has yielded rewarding results that help others. Dr. Pesce recounts a project in which his team developed a way of examining cancer in mice. He received a letter commending him on the work from a colleague working in cancer research and feels greatly rewarded to know that someone thinks highly enough of his team's work to build on their results.

Another of the team's accomplishments involved devising a way to cut the cost of drugs used to treat transplant patients from $6,000 a year to $1,200. With this reduction in cost, third world countries can afford the drugs, which was not possible before.

Dr. Pesce advises that a Ph.D. is essential to a successful research career. He also credits having an understanding partner with adding to his success. In addition, he says, "Because it is so important to be able to interact with people, exchange ideas, and get them to help with particular areas of your project, you must have the ability to get along with all kinds of people. You have to be aware of what issues others have and be able to accommodate them so they'll accommodate you in return. I have found that this is the proper approach to a successful collaboration. It's not unlike working with others on a book or any other project in which a number of people need to extend themselves in order to fulfill a common goal."

H. Graham Purchase, Ph.D., Veterinary Medical Researcher

Dr. Purchase is the director of veterinary medical research at Mississippi State University. He was born in Rhodesia (now Zimbabwe), educated in Kenya, and received his university training in South Africa. Following the advice of his father, also a veterinarian who worked in research, Dr. Purchase earned a bachelor's degree in botany in order to learn about the animal world before starting veterinary school. After receiving his veterinary degree in South Africa, he practiced there for two years before fulfilling his dream of coming to the United States to work in research. Once here, he earned a master's degree and a doctorate in microbiology and public health from Michigan State University.

Dr. Purchase started his research work in a poultry laboratory in East Lansing, Michigan, where he worked for thirteen years performing research on tumor viruses of poultry species. He describes this period as being at the right place at the right time, because the lab discovered the cause of Marek's disease, one of the most economically devastating poultry diseases in the world. The lab staff developed a vaccine to prevent the disease. It was the first commercially applicable cancer vaccine ever developed and is now used worldwide. "This period was the most exciting and rewarding of my life," says Dr. Purchase.

As a bench researcher (one who works in a laboratory), Dr. Purchase examined the cultures of cells in which disease-causing viruses or the vaccine that prevented them were grown. He would routinely isolate birds that had died in the experiments and open them to examine what they died from to verify that it was the challenge and not something else unrelated to the experiment. He also spent time writing manuscripts and grant proposals, work that he often took home to complete because there wasn't enough time during the day.

After thirteen years at the laboratory, Dr. Purchase moved into administration and was offered a job in Washington, D.C. He spent the next fourteen years in nine different jobs in research administration, working in plant, animal, and human nutrition; family economics; soil; and water. But because his primary interest is in veterinary research, Dr. Purchase was happy to accept a position at Mississippi State University's College of Veterinary Medicine. The research performed there is on the prime commodities of Mississippi, which include poultry, its number one product, and catfish, one of the state's biggest income producers.

Working as a research administrator, a typical day for Dr. Purchase involves interacting one-on-one with many individuals. Because he handles the budget of the college, he is often busy with budget forms and various commitment forms, such as travel allowances, equipment purchases, and hiring decisions. He also reviews manuscripts and grant proposals from the department staff. The college is accredited by the American Association for the Accreditation of Laboratory Animal Care, which maintains very high standards of review for all experiments on animals. Every single experiment that involves animals has to be reviewed by an animal care and use committee to make sure that the animals are not harmed unnecessarily. The accreditation also involves making sure that the facilities are properly maintained, which is another of Dr. Purchase's responsibilities.

A large part of the day is spent in meetings with superiors to keep them abreast of how the research projects are progressing. Dr. Purchase prepares reports on current research projects, most of which are for the general use of administrators and legislators. The research is written up by the faculty of the college and submitted for peer review to ensure that the conclusions are supported by the data. Dr. Purchase oversees this review process. He also frequently escorts visitors through the college's research facilities.

There are several levels of researchers working at the College of Veterinary Medicine. In most cases, the principal investigators who design the experiments and lead the teams have doctoral degrees. The college employs many technicians, who have master's and bachelor's degrees. Some of the animal caretakers and technicians have technician degrees; others are high school graduates. There are also students working toward bachelor's degrees who gain experience by doing laboratory clean-up work. Graduate students working toward their master's or doctoral degrees spend a good deal of time with their major professors, learning how to conduct experiments and do research.

Based on his years of experience, Dr. Purchase can offer some good advice about a career in research. "If your grades are good, if you perform well during examinations, and if you can become an expert in these areas, research is a wonderful career," he says. "It's challenging and very innovative. I enjoy being able to develop something and to find out new things. But it's very rigorous, too. Most of my researchers are not here from nine to five. They're here early in the morning, they frequently miss their lunch breaks, and they take work home at night or come in at night and weekends to keep their work going. Research means pushing forward the frontiers of science, and to succeed, you must be trained, prepared, and dedicated to putting in the necessary hours and effort."

Michael S. Shanler, Engineering Researcher

Michael S. Shanler is an engineering research associate at the Genetics Institute, Small Molecule Drug Discovery, in Cambridge, Massachusetts. He received his bachelor of science degree in biomedical engineering from Boston University and is working toward a master's degree in business administration at Northeastern University in Boston. He has also received Oracle OCP Database training and Zymark Robotics training.

Michael got his job with the Genetics Institute through a temp agency and was hired for a full-time position and promoted after three months. His job involves the study of preclinical drug candidates, laboratory automation, and computer modeling. He enjoys the challenging work, especially because he feels that it benefits society.

Michael's father was an engineer with a master's degree in business administration, so he sees himself as following in his dad's footsteps to a degree. He knew that he wanted to earn an engineering degree but preferred something less mainstream. This led to his focus on biomedical research, which he pursued because he enjoys problem solving and wanted to apply what he'd learned in college before beginning graduate school. Michael initially worked in pharmaceutical production after college but found the work monotonous. Now that he's redirected his focus to drug research, his work is more challenging and rewarding.

Michael describes his work atmosphere as enjoyable and spends a good deal of time engaged in worthwhile discussions. The staff works hard all week but can relax a bit on Fridays. Although the work isn't dangerous, they must use caution when working with chemicals, biological materials, and radiation. Michael usually works about forty hours a week. He spends about fifteen hours working with robotics and another fifteen hours on analysis of his work. He spends about five hours on collaborative projects and bench research, and the rest of the time is spent in meetings and seminars.

One of the things Michael enjoys most is his autonomy in his research position. Although he's held accountable for his work, he is free to set his own hours, write his own protocols, and collaborate on projects. What he likes least is not having a structured day, because it's sometimes easy to be lured into taking time off.

"To others interested in entering this line of work, I would say that you shouldn't be afraid of making career-changing decisions," Michael advises. "As soon as a job situation becomes stale, it is time to start hunting for another one. Life is too short to spend time being bored or suffering through mundane work."

Dennis J. Ernst, Medical Technologist

Dennis J. Ernst is director of the Center for Phlebotomy Education. He is a medical technologist, certified by the American Society of Clinical Pathologists since 1978. He describes his start in the field and his job as a clinical microbiologist at the University of Louisville Hospital in Louisville, Kentucky. "How I got started may be broken down into two parts—what attracted me to a career in the health sciences and what attracted me to a career as a medical technologist," Dennis says. "The answers are completely different and say as much about the educational process as they do my impatience with it."

Dennis's mother was a registered nurse, and his earliest memories were inspired by her dedication to caring for the sick and the satisfaction she received from her work. "I came to know that caring for the sick was a noble and rewarding thing. I saw her as someone who had been blessed by fate to see and know the inner workings of the human body, and for me to be so blessed when I came of age was an intriguing prospect."

Dennis studied science in high school and enrolled in the premed program at Albion College in Albion, Michigan. Unfortunately, Dennis's scores on the science placement exam that he took during his first week of classes indicated that he was unlikely to succeed in premed. In addition, his advisor informed him that he was poorly prepared to major in any science curriculum.

Dennis was stunned by this news and felt that if he could not major in science, he didn't want to be in school at all. He describes himself as "too ignorant to take his advice and too stubborn to pursue another major." With this attitude, Dennis decided to prove both the advisor and the placement tests wrong. He majored in biology but only had mediocre grades, far below what he needed to enter medical school. Although he was still interested in science, his grade point average eliminated medical school and most other high-profile careers.

"By now the struggle had been long and hard, and I was wearing thin on persistence," Dennis recalls. "I had experienced enough of education but still needed to emerge with a face-saving career of some security. The allied health fields presented many offerings, but most of them required more postgraduate study than I had the will to endure. Then my advisor recommended medical technology, the study of blood and disease. It was perfect! I could get that inside peek at the inner workings of the human body that I still craved and with only one year of postgraduate study. I applied for internships and was accepted."

Medical technology involves the laboratory testing of body fluids and tissues for disease. The field includes many subcategories, all of which Dennis has worked at in varying degrees. As a clinical microbiologist in a university hospital, he tests blood, tissues, and body fluids for microorganisms that cause infection. He identifies the microorganisms and recommends antibiotics to fight them. His work also includes immunology, which is research to detect the presence of disease-fighting antibodies.

Dennis works four eight-hour days a week. A typical day begins with retrieving and collating data that is printed by an automated instrument that works throughout the night to identify microorganisms by species. The data is obtained from patient cultures isolated the previous day. After identification, technologists determine the best antibiotic therapy to be used against the particular organism. Dennis enters the collated information into the hospital computer system and phones any life-threatening results to the appropriate physician for immediate treatment. He then sets up newly isolated organisms for the same automated, overnight testing. Dennis is also responsible for the maintenance of his automated equipment and for quality control processes that assure his analytical systems are functioning properly.

Working as a clinical microbiologist carries the risk of infection, but this is minimized with the proper and consistent use of personal protective devices such as gowns, gloves, and face shields. Dennis says that the work can be hectic when the hospital is full, but there are times when the patient population is low and the work is light. Overtime is not permitted, so any time spent working more than his scheduled hours must be offset by working proportionally less on another day.

Nearly all of Dennis's coworkers at the hospital have either associate's or bachelor's degrees, and all are certified laboratory professionals in some capacity. The laboratory assistants who prepare the specimens for bacterial isolation and perform many nontechnical tasks are high school graduates who have received on-the-job training.

Dennis describes the most satisfying aspect of his work as the collaboration that exists among his colleagues. He describes both the level of cooperation and the department's goal-oriented momentum as high.

"Anyone interested in a career in the allied health sciences should consider medical technology for the insights it offers into the inner workings of the human body," Dennis says. "Here one finds the constant discovery of the body's beauty and complexity that I hungered for as the young, observant son of a nurse. The intrigue has never ceased. Applications of the skills learned in training are many and varied, rendering the possibility of job burnout in this career remote. However, because of the sweeping application of managed care strategies in health care today, medical technology as a career has changed from one of promised permanence to one that is, at best, a stepping-stone to a more secure and respected calling."

For More Information

For information on careers in the biological sciences, contact:

American Institute of Biological Sciences
1444 I Street NW, Suite 200
Washington, DC 20005
www.aibs.org

Canadian Federation of Biological Societies
305-1750 Courtwood Crescent
Ottawa, ON K2C 2B5
Canada
www.cfbs.org

For information on careers in physiology, contact:

American Physiological Society
Education Office
9650 Rockville Pike
Bethesda, MD 20814
www.the-aps.org

For information on careers in biotechnology, contact:

Biotechnology Industry Organization
1225 Eye Street NW, Suite 400
Washington, DC 20005
www.bio.org

For information on careers in biochemistry, contact:

American Society for Biochemistry and Molecular Biology
9650 Rockville Pike
Bethesda, MD 20814
www.asbmb.org

Canadian Society of Biochemistry, Molecular and Cellular
  Biology
305-1750 Courtwood Crescent
Ottawa, ON K2C 2B5
Canada
www.csbmcb.ca

For information on careers in biophysics, contact:

Biophysical Society
9650 Rockville Pike, Room 0512
Bethesda, MD 20814
www.biophysics.org

For information on careers in botany, contact:

Botanical Society of America
PO Box 299
St. Louis, MO 63166
www.botany.org

For information on careers in microbiology, contact:

American Society for Microbiology
1752 N Street NW
Washington, DC 20036
www.asm.org

Canadian Society of Microbiologists
375 West Fifth Avenue, Suite 201
Vancouver, BC V5Y 1J6
Canada
www.csm-scm.org

Information on acquiring a job as a biological or medical scientist with the federal government may be obtained from the Office of Personnel Management. Visit the official website at www.usajobs.com for details.

In Canada, visit the website at www.jobs-emplois.gc.ca for federal job postings.

CHAPTER THREE

Careers in the Physical Sciences

Lucky is he who has been able to understand
the causes of things.
—Virgil

D id you know that studying balloons can lead to great discoveries? Have you ever heard of Charles's law? It states that the volume of a given mass of gas at constant pressure is directly proportional to its absolute temperature (in kelvin). The law is attributed to the work of Jacques Charles (1746–1823), a French physicist who studied gases and made his first ascent in a hydrogen-filled balloon in 1783. Upon hearing about the hot-air balloons of the French Montgolfier brothers, Charles and his brothers began experimenting with hydrogen balloons. Incredibly, they made their ascent only ten days after the Montgolfiers' first flight. Charles's work on the expansion of gases led to the formulation of the 1787 law that bears his name.

Physical Scientists

Physical scientists serve as investigators, continually involved in a never-ending search to learn more about the laws that govern our universe.

Chemists

A chemist's goal is to search for new knowledge about chemicals and put it to practical use. Although chemicals are often thought of as artificial or toxic substances, they are part of the composition of all physical things, whether naturally occurring or of human design.

Chemists have developed a tremendous variety of new and improved synthetic fibers: paints, adhesives, drugs, cosmetics, electronic components, lubricants, and thousands of other products. They also develop processes that save energy and reduce pollution, such as improved oil refining and petrochemical processing methods. Research on the chemistry of living things spurs advances in medicine, agriculture, food processing, and other areas.

Many chemists work in research and development. Those involved in basic research investigate the properties, composition, and structure of matter and the laws that govern the combination of elements and reactions of substances. In applied research and development, they create new products and processes or improve existing ones, often using knowledge gained from basic research. For example, synthetic rubber and plastics resulted from research on small molecules uniting to form large ones (polymerization).

Chemists also work in production and quality control in chemical manufacturing plants. They prepare instructions that specify ingredients, mixing times, and temperatures for each stage in the process. They also monitor automated processes to ensure proper product yield, and they test samples to ensure they meet industry and government standards. Chemists also record and report on test results. Some serve as marketing or sales representatives who sell and provide technical information on chemical products.

Many chemists specialize in a subfield. For instance, analytical chemists determine the structure, composition, and nature of substances and develop analytical techniques. They also identify the presence and concentration of chemical pollutants in air, water, and soil. Organic chemists study the chemistry of the vast number of carbon compounds. Their work has led to the development of many commercial products, such as drugs, plastics, and fertilizers. Inorganic chemists study compounds consisting mainly of elements other than carbon, such as those in electronic components. Physical chemists study the characteristics of atoms and molecules and investigate how chemical reactions work. Their research may result in new and better energy sources.

Chemists who work in production and quality control test samples to ensure that product specifications are met.

Physicists

Physicists explore and identify basic principles governing the structure and behavior of matter, the generation and transfer of energy, and the interaction of matter and energy. Some use these principles in theoretical areas, such as the nature of time and the origin of the universe; others apply their physics knowledge to practical areas, such as the development of advanced materials, electronic and optical devices, and medical equipment.

Physicists design and perform experiments with lasers, cyclotrons, telescopes, mass spectrometers, and other equipment. Based on observation and analysis, they attempt to discover the laws that describe the forces of nature, such as gravity, electromagnetism, and nuclear interactions. They also find ways to apply physical laws and theories to problems in nuclear energy, electronics, optics, materials, communications, aerospace technology, navigation equipment, and medical instrumentation.

Most physicists work in research and development. Some do basic research to increase scientific knowledge; others conduct applied research to build upon the discoveries made through basic research and work to develop new devices, products, and processes. For instance, basic research in solid-state physics led to the development of transistors and then to the integrated circuits used in computers.

Physicists also design research equipment that often has additional unanticipated uses. For example, lasers are used in surgery; microwave devices are used for ovens; and measuring instruments can analyze blood or the chemical content of foods. A small number of physicists work in inspection, testing, quality control, and other production-related jobs in industry.

Much physics research is done in small or midsize laboratories. However, experiments in plasma, nuclear energy, high energy, and some other areas of physics require extremely large, expensive equipment, such as particle accelerators, and physicists in these subfields often work in large teams. Although physics research may require extensive experimentation in laboratories, research physicists still spend time in offices planning, recording, analyzing, and reporting on research.

Physicists generally specialize in one of many subfields—elementary particle physics, nuclear physics, atomic and molecular physics, physics of condensed matter (solid-state physics), optics, acoustics, plasma physics, or the physics of fluids. Some specialize in a subdivision of one of these subfields; for example, within condensed matter physics, specialties include superconductivity, crystallography, and semiconductors. However, since all areas of physics involve the same fundamental principles, specialties may overlap, and physicists may switch from one subfield to another. Also, growing numbers of physicists work in combined fields such as biophysics, chemical physics, and geophysics.

Astronomers

Astronomy is sometimes considered a subfield of physics because astronomers use the principles of physics and mathematics to learn about the fundamental nature of the universe, including the sun, moon, planets, stars, and galaxies. They also apply their knowledge to problems in navigation and space flight.

Almost all astronomers conduct research. They analyze large quantities of data gathered by observatories and satellites and write scientific papers or reports on their findings. Most spend only a few weeks each year making observations with optical telescopes, radio telescopes, and other instruments. Contrary to the popular image, astronomers almost never make observations by looking directly through a telescope because enhanced photographic and electronic detecting equipment can see more than the human eye.

Geologists and Geophysicists

Geologists and geophysicists, also known as geological scientists or geoscientists, study the physical aspects and history of the earth. They identify and examine rocks, study information collected by remote sensing instruments in satellites, conduct geological surveys, construct maps, and use instruments to measure the earth's gravity and magnetic field. They also analyze information collected through seismic studies, which involves bouncing energy waves off buried rock layers. Many search for oil, natural gas, minerals, and groundwater.

Other geoscientists play an important role in preserving and cleaning up the environment. Their activities include designing and monitoring waste disposal sites, preserving water supplies, and reclaiming contaminated land and water to comply with federal environmental regulations. They also help locate safe sites for hazardous waste facilities and landfills.

Geologists and geophysicists examine chemical and physical properties of specimens in laboratories. They study fossil remains of animal and plant life or experiment with the flow of water and oil through rocks. Geoscientists sometimes use two- or three-dimensional computer modeling to portray water layers and the flow of water or other fluids through rock cracks and porous materials. They use a variety of sophisticated laboratory instruments, including x-ray diffractometers, which determine the crystal structure of minerals, and petrographic microscopes, for the study of rock and sediment samples. Seismographs, instruments that measure energy waves resulting from movements in the earth's crust, are also used to determine the locations and intensities of earthquakes.

Geoscientists working in the oil and gas industry sometimes process and interpret the maps produced by remote-sensing satellites to help identify potential new oil or gas deposits. Seismic technology is another important exploration tool. Seismic waves are used to develop three-dimensional computer models of underground or underwater rock formations.

These scientists also apply geological knowledge to engineering problems in constructing buildings, dams, tunnels, and highways. Some administer and manage research and exploration programs; others become general managers working for petroleum or mining companies.

Although geology and geophysics are closely related fields, there are major differences. Geologists study the composition, structure, and history of the earth's crust, trying to find out how rocks were formed and what has happened to them since their formation. Geophysicists use the principles of physics and mathematics to study not only the earth's surface but its internal composition, ground and surface waters, atmosphere, and oceans as well as its magnetic, electrical, and gravitational forces. Both, however, commonly apply their skills to the search for natural resources and to solving environmental problems.

There are numerous subdisciplines or specialties under these two major disciplines that further differentiate the kind of work geoscientists do. For example, petroleum geologists explore for oil and gas deposits by studying and mapping the subsurface of the ocean or land. They use sophisticated geophysical instrumentation and computers to collect information. Mineralogists analyze and classify minerals and precious stones according to composition and structure. Paleontologists study fossils found in geological formations to trace the evolution of plant and animal life and the geologic history of the earth. Stratigraphers help to locate minerals by studying the distribution and arrangement of sedimentary rock layers and by examining the fossil and mineral content of such layers. Those who study marine geology are usually called oceanographers or marine geologists. They study and map the ocean floor and collect information using remote-sensing devices aboard surface ships or underwater research craft.

Geophysicists may specialize in areas such as geodesy, seismology, or marine geophysics, also known as physical oceanography. Geodesists study the size and shape of the earth, its gravitational field, tides, polar motion, and rotation. Seismologists interpret data from seismographs and other geophysical instruments to detect earthquakes and locate earthquake-related faults. Physical oceanographers study the physical aspects of oceans, such as currents and the interaction of sea surface and atmosphere.

Hydrology is a discipline closely related to geology and geophysics. Hydrologists study the distribution, circulation, and physical properties of underground and surface waters in order to understand the form and intensity of precipitation, its rate of infiltration into the soil, its movement through the earth, and its return to the ocean and atmosphere. The work they do is particularly important in environmental preservation and remediation.

Meteorologists

Meteorology is the study of the atmosphere, the air that covers the earth. Meteorologists study the atmosphere's physical characteristics, motions, and processes, and the way the atmosphere affects the rest of our environment. The best-known application of this knowledge is in forecasting the weather, although weather information and meteorological research also are applied in air-pollution control, agriculture, air and sea transportation, defense, and the study of trends in the earth's climate, such as global warming or ozone depletion.

Meteorologists who forecast the weather, known professionally as operational meteorologists, are the largest group of specialists. They study information on air pressure, temperature, humidity, and wind velocity and apply physical and mathematical relationships to make short- and long-range weather forecasts. Their data come from weather satellites, weather radar, and remote sensors and observers in many parts of the world. Meteorologists use sophisticated computer models of the world's atmosphere to make long-term, short-term, and local forecasts. These forecasts inform not only the general public but also those who need accurate weather information for both economic and safety reasons, as in the shipping, aviation, agriculture, fishing, and utilities industries.

The use of weather balloons to measure wind, temperature, and humidity in the upper atmosphere is supplemented by far more sophisticated weather equipment that transmits data as frequently as every few minutes. Doppler radar, for example, can detect rotational patterns in violent storm systems, allowing forecasters to better predict thunderstorms, tornadoes, and flash floods, as well as their direction and intensity.

Some meteorologists work in research. Physical meteorologists, for example, study the atmosphere's chemical and physical properties; the transmission of light, sound, and radio waves; and the transfer of energy in the atmosphere. They also study factors affecting formation of clouds, rain, snow, and other weather phenomena, such as severe storms. Climatologists collect, analyze, and interpret past records of wind, rainfall, sunshine, and temperature in specific areas or regions. Their studies are used to design buildings and to plan heating and cooling systems, to aid in effective land use, and in agricultural production. Other research meteorologists examine the most effective ways to control or diminish air pollution or improve weather forecasting using mathematical models.

Jobs in weather stations, most of which operate around the clock seven days a week, often involve night, weekend, and holiday work and rotating shifts. Overtime may be required during times of weather emergencies, such as hurricanes. Operational meteorologists are also often under pressure to meet forecast deadlines. Weather stations are found all over the country: in airports, in or near cities, and in isolated and remote areas.

Some meteorologists also spend time observing weather conditions and collecting data from aircraft. Meteorologists in smaller weather offices often work alone, while those working in larger offices often operate as part of a team. Those who work for private consulting firms or for companies that analyze and monitor emissions to improve air quality often work with other science or engineering professionals.

Education and Training

Each of the physical sciences has its own education and training requirements. Keep reading to see whether you'd like to pursue one of these challenging fields.

Chemists

You need at least a bachelor's degree in chemistry or a related discipline to work as a chemist. For most research jobs, however, a doctoral degree is the minimum requirement. Many colleges and universities offer bachelor's degree programs in chemistry, and a large number are approved by the American Chemical Society. Several hundred also offer advanced degree programs.

If you are planning a career as a chemist, you should enjoy studying science and mathematics and should like working with your hands building scientific apparatuses and performing experiments. In addition to required courses in analytical, inorganic, organic, and physical chemistry, the undergraduate program includes courses in biological sciences, mathematics, and physics. Computer courses are invaluable, as employers increasingly prefer job applicants to be not only computer literate but able to apply computer skills to modeling and simulation tasks. Laboratory instruments are also computerized, and the ability to operate and understand equipment is a necessity. Perseverance, curiosity, and the ability to concentrate on detail and to work independently are also essential.

Because chemists who engage in research and development are increasingly expected to work on interdisciplinary teams, you need some understanding of other disciplines, including business and marketing or economics, along with leadership ability and good oral and written communication skills. Any experience you can gain in academic laboratories or through internships or co-op programs in industry is also useful. Several years of postdoctoral experience are preferred by some employers, particularly those in the pharmaceutical industry.

Although graduate students typically specialize in a subfield of chemistry, such as analytical chemistry or polymer chemistry, you usually don't need to specialize at the undergraduate level. In fact, as an undergraduate with broad training, you'll have more flexibility when job hunting or changing jobs than if you narrowly define your interests. Most employers provide new bachelor's degree chemists with additional training or education.

If you'd like to work in government or industry, your bachelor's degree will qualify you for jobs in technical sales or services, quality control, or as assistant senior chemist in research and development laboratories. You may also be qualified to work in research positions, analyzing and testing products, but these are likely to be technicians' positions with limited upward mobility.

You should keep in mind that many employers prefer chemists who work in basic and applied research to have doctorates, and a doctorate is also generally preferred for advancement to many administrative positions. Many chemists who work in sales, marketing, or professional research positions eventually move into management.

A bachelor's degree in chemistry is also a good background for entry into other occupations, such as technical writing or chemical marketing. It can also be a solid basis if you plan to enter medical, dental, veterinary, or other health profession schools.

As a chemistry graduate, you may also become a high school teacher; you may teach at the college or university level if you have a doctorate. A degree in chemistry may also qualify you to work as an engineer, especially if you've taken some courses in chemical engineering.

Physicists and Astronomers

Because most jobs are in research and development, a doctoral degree is the usual educational requirement for physicists and astronomers, many of whom ultimately take jobs teaching at the college or university level. Although it's not required, additional experience and training in a postdoctoral research assignment is helpful in preparing for permanent research positions.

A bachelor's or master's degree in physics is rarely adequate for work as a physicist, but either would usually qualify for work as a technician or an assistant in laboratories in engineering-related or other scientific fields. You may also be qualified for applied research jobs in private industry or nonresearch positions in the federal government. A master's degree often suffices for teaching jobs in two-year colleges. Many graduates with bachelor's degrees in astronomy enter an unrelated field, but they are also qualified to work in planetariums running science shows or to assist astronomers doing research.

Hundreds of colleges and universities offer bachelor's degree programs in physics. An undergraduate program provides a broad background in the natural sciences and mathematics and typically includes courses in mechanics, atomic physics, electromagnetism, thermodynamics, optics, and quantum mechanics.

Approximately 185 colleges and universities have departments offering doctoral degrees in physics; an additional 68 offer a master's as their highest degree in physics. Graduate students usually concentrate in a subfield of physics, such as elementary particles or condensed matter, and many begin studying for their doctorate immediately after receiving their bachelor's degree.

About eighty universities grant degrees in astronomy, either through an astronomy, physics, or combined physics-astronomy department. With fewer than forty doctoral programs in astronomy, you should be prepared to face considerable competition for available slots—a very strong physics background will be helpful in securing a place. In fact, an undergraduate degree in either physics or astronomy is excellent preparation.

You need strong mathematical ability, computer skills, an inquisitive mind, imagination, and the ability to work independently to have a successful career in physics or astronomy. If you hope to work in industrial laboratories applying physics knowledge to practical problems, you should broaden your educational background to include courses outside of physics, such as economics, computer technology, and current affairs. Good oral and written communication skills are also important because many physicists work as part of a team or have contact with clients or customers with nonphysics backgrounds.

As a physics or astronomy doctoral graduate, your first job will likely be conducting research in a postdoctoral position, where you may work with experienced physicists as they continue to learn about their specialties and develop ideas and results to be used in later work. The initial work may be routine and remain under the close supervision of senior scientists. After some experience, you'll perform more complex tasks and work more independently. Physicists who develop new products or processes sometimes form their own companies or join new firms to exploit their own ideas.

Geologists and Geophysicists

A bachelor's degree in geology or geophysics is adequate for entry into some lower-level geology jobs, but you need at least a master's degree for better jobs with good advancement potential. A strong background in physics, chemistry, mathematics, or computer science may qualify you for some jobs. A doctorate is required for most research positions in colleges and universities and is also important for work in federal agencies and some state geological surveys that involve basic research.

More than one hundred universities offer accredited bachelor's degree programs in geoscience, including geology, geophysics, and oceanography. About eighty universities have master's degree programs, and about sixty offer doctoral degree programs. The curriculum includes traditional geoscience courses emphasizing classical geologic methods and topics (such as mineralogy, paleontology, stratigraphy, and structural geology). However, if you are interested in working in the environmental or regulatory fields, you should also take courses in hydrology, hazardous waste management, environmental legislation, chemistry, mechanics, and geologic logging. Since some employers seek applicants with field experience, a summer internship or employment in an environmentally related area may be beneficial as well.

It is important for you to be capable of working as part of a team. You also need strong skills in computer modeling, data processing, and effective oral and written communication, as well as the ability to think independently and creatively. Physical stamina is a must for jobs involving fieldwork.

It is likely that your career will begin with field exploration or working as a laboratory research assistant. As you gain experience, you'll be given more difficult assignments and eventually may be promoted to project leader, program manager, or another management or research position.

Meteorologists

A bachelor's degree with a major in meteorology or a closely related field with course work in meteorology is the usual minimum requirement for a beginning job as a meteorologist.

The federal government prefers to hire entry-level meteorologists with bachelor's degrees, not necessarily in meteorology, with at least twenty-four semester hours of meteorology courses, including six hours in the analysis and prediction of weather systems, six hours of atmospheric dynamics and thermodynamics, three hours of physical meteorology, and two hours of remote sensing of the atmosphere or instrumentation.

Other required courses include three semester hours of ordinary differential equations, six hours of college physics, and at least nine hours of courses appropriate for a physical science major—such as statistics, chemistry, physical oceanography, physical climatology, physical hydrology, radiative transfer, aeronomy, advanced thermodynamics, advanced electricity and magnetism, light and optics, and computer science. Sometimes, a combination of education and experience may be substituted for a degree.

While you may be qualified for positions in operational meteorology with only a bachelor's degree, obtaining a graduate degree will enhance your advancement potential. A master's degree is usually necessary for conducting research and development, and a doctorate may be required for some research positions.

If you are planning a career in research and development, you don't necessarily have to major in meteorology as an undergraduate. In fact, a bachelor's degree in either mathematics, physics, or engineering is excellent preparation for graduate study in meteorology.

Because atmospheric science is a small field, relatively few colleges and universities offer degrees in meteorology or atmospheric science, although many departments of physics, earth science, geography, and geophysics offer atmospheric science and related courses. In 2005, the American Meteorological Society (AMS) approved approximately one hundred undergraduate and graduate atmospheric science programs, many of which combine the study of meteorology with another field, such as agriculture, hydrology, oceanography, engineering, or physics. For example, hydrometeorology is the blending of hydrology (the science of the earth's water) and meteorology and is the field concerned with the effect of precipitation on the hydrologic cycle and the environment.

As a beginning meteorologist, you'd likely do routine data collection, computation, or analysis and some basic forecasting. If you work at an entry-level position in the federal government, you'd generally be placed in an intern position for training and experience.

Once you've gained experience, you may advance to various supervisory or administrative jobs or may handle more complex forecasting jobs. Increasing numbers of meteorologists establish their own weather consulting services.

Job Outlook

If you're intrigued by these careers in the physical sciences, read on to see what the job outlook is for the next few years.

Chemists

Employment of chemists is expected to grow only as much as 8 percent through 2014, which is slower than the anticipated rate for all occupations. Pharmaceutical and medicine manufacturing and professional, scientific, and technical services firms will account for most of the job growth.

Employment in the nonpharmaceutical segments of the chemical industry, a major employer of chemists, is expected to decline over the projection period. This means that new chemists at all levels may experience competition for jobs in these areas, including basic chemical manufacturing and synthetic materials.

Graduates with bachelor's degrees should find science-related jobs in sales, marketing, and middle management, as well as positions as chemical technicians or technologists or high school chemistry teachers. An increasing number of bachelor's degree holders are finding assistant research positions at smaller research organizations.

Graduates with master's degrees, and particularly those with doctorates, will enjoy better opportunities at larger pharmaceutical and biotechnology firms. Those with advanced degrees will continue to fill most senior research and upper management positions, although applicants are likely to experience competition for these jobs.

Within the chemical industry, job opportunities are expected to be most plentiful in pharmaceutical and biotechnology firms. Biotechnological research, including studies of human genes, continues to offer possibilities for the development of new drugs and products to combat illnesses and diseases that have previously been unresponsive to treatments derived by traditional chemical processes. Stronger competition among drug companies and an aging population are contributing to the need for new drugs.

Employment in the remaining segments of the chemical industry is expected to decline as companies downsize. To control costs, most chemical companies will increasingly turn to scientific research and development services firms to perform specialized research and other work formerly done by in-house chemists. As a result, these firms will experience healthy growth. Quality control will continue to be an important issue in chemical manufacturing and other industries that use chemicals in their manufacturing processes.

Chemists also will be needed to develop and improve the technologies and processes used to produce chemicals for all purposes and to monitor and measure air and water pollutants to ensure compliance with local, state, and federal environmental regulations. Environmental research should offer many new opportunities for chemists and materials scientists. To satisfy public concerns and to comply with government regulations, the chemical industry will continue to invest billions of dollars each year in technology that reduces pollution and cleans up existing waste sites. Chemists also are needed to find ways to use less energy and to discover alternative sources of energy.

Layoffs may occur during periods of economic recession, especially in the industrial chemicals industry. Layoffs are less likely in the pharmaceutical industry, where long development cycles generally overshadow short-term economic effects. The traditional chemical industry, however, provides many raw materials to the auto manufacturing and construction industries, both of which are vulnerable to temporary slowdowns during recessions.

Physicists and Astronomers

The U.S. Bureau of Labor Statistics states that employment of physicists and astronomers is expected to grow only as much as 8 percent through 2014. This low growth rate can be attributed to the fact that federal research expenditures are the major source of research funds for physics and astronomy, and the limited amount of available science research funds will result in competition for basic research jobs among Ph.D. holders. Most expected job openings will occur as a result of the need to replace physicists and astronomers who retire or leave the occupation for other reasons.

Although research and development expenditures in private industry should continue to grow, many private research laboratories are expected to continue to reduce basic research in favor of applied or manufacturing research and product and software development. Despite this, those with a physics background should continue to be in demand in the areas of information technology, semiconductor technology, and other applied sciences; however, many new workers may have job titles such as computer software engineer, computer programmer, systems analyst, or developer, rather than physicist.

Throughout the 1990s, the number of doctorates granted in physics was much greater than the number of job openings for physicists, resulting in keen competition, particularly for research positions in colleges and universities and in research and development centers. Recent increases in undergraduate physics enrollments may lead to growth in enrollments in graduate physics programs, which may further increase the number of doctoral degrees granted, intensifying the competition for job openings.

Opportunities may be more numerous for those with master's degrees, particularly graduates from programs preparing students for applied research and development, product design, and manufacturing positions in private industry. Many of these positions, however, will have titles other than physicist, such as engineer or computer scientist.

Graduates with only a bachelor's degree in physics or astronomy are not qualified for most research jobs, but they may qualify for a wide range of positions related to engineering, mathematics, computer science, and environmental science. Those with the appropriate background may be qualified for positions in some nonscience fields, such as finance.

Those graduates who meet state certification requirements can become high school physics teachers, an occupation in strong demand in many school districts. Most states require new teachers to obtain a master's degree in education within a certain time period. Although competition is high for traditional physics and astronomy research jobs, graduates with a physics or astronomy degree at any level will find their knowledge of science and mathematics useful for entry into many other occupations.

Geologists and Geophysicists

Although employment growth will vary by occupational specialty, overall employment of geoscientists is expected to grow up to

8 percent through 2014. Due to the relatively low number of qualified geoscience graduates and the large number of expected retirements, opportunities are expected to be good in most areas of geoscience.

Graduates with master's degrees may have the best opportunities, while those with doctorates who wish to become college and university faculty or to do advanced research may face competition. There are few openings for graduates with only a bachelor's degree in geoscience, but these graduates may find excellent opportunities as high school science teachers. They also can become science technicians or enter a wide variety of related occupations.

Many geologists and geophysicists work in the exploration and production of oil and gas. Historically, employment of petroleum geologists and geophysicists has been cyclical and affected considerably by the price of oil and gas. When prices were low, oil and gas producers curtailed exploration activities and laid off geologists. When prices were higher, companies had the funds and incentive to renew exploration efforts and hire geoscientists in larger numbers. In recent years, a growing worldwide demand for oil and gas and for new exploration and recovery techniques, particularly in deep water and previously inaccessible sites in Alaska and the Gulf of Mexico, has returned some stability to the petroleum industry. Growth in this area, though, will be limited due to increasing efficiencies in finding oil and gas. Geoscientists who speak a foreign language and who are willing to work abroad should enjoy the best opportunities, as the need for energy, construction materials, and a broad range of geoscience expertise grows in developing nations.

Job growth is expected within management, scientific, and technical consulting services, where demand will be spurred by a continuing emphasis on the need for energy, environmental protection, responsible land management, and water-related issues. These services have increased their hiring of many geoscientists in recent years due to increased government contracting, and also in response to demand for professionals to provide technical assistance and management plans to corporations. The need to monitor the quality of the environment, including aquatic ecosystems, issues related to water conservation, deteriorating coastal environments, and rising sea levels will stimulate employment growth of geoscientists.

An expected increase in highway building and other infrastructure projects will be a source of jobs for engineering geologists.

Few opportunities for geoscientists are expected in federal and state government, mostly because of budgetary constraints at key agencies and the trend among governments toward contracting out to consulting firms. However, departures of geoscientists who retire or leave the government for other reasons will result in some job openings over the next decade.

A small number of new jobs should result from the need for oceanographers to conduct research for the military or for federal agencies such as the National Oceanic and Atmospheric Administration (NOAA) on issues related to maintaining healthy and productive oceans.

During periods of economic recession, geoscientists may be laid off. Especially vulnerable to layoffs are those in consulting and, to a lesser extent, workers in government. Employment for those working in the production of oil and gas, however, will largely be dictated by the cyclical nature of the energy sector and changes in government policy.

Meteorologists

Over the next several years, job opportunities for meteorologists are expected to be better in private industry than in the federal government. There are two reasons for this projection. First, the National Weather Service has completed an extensive modernization of its weather forecasting equipment and has no plans to increase the number of weather stations or the number of meteorologists in existing stations. Employment of meteorologists in other federal agencies is expected to remain stable.

Second, as research leads to continuing improvements in weather forecasting, demand should grow for private weather consulting firms to provide more detailed information than has formerly been available, especially to climate-sensitive industries. Farmers, commodity investors, radio and television stations, and utilities, transportation, and construction firms can greatly benefit from additional weather information more closely targeted to their needs than the general information provided by the National Weather Service.

Additionally, research on seasonal and other long-range forecasting is yielding positive results, which should spur demand for more meteorologists to interpret these forecasts and advise climate-sensitive industries. However, the sales and growth of private weather services depend on the health of the economy, since many of the customers are in industries sensitive to fluctuations in the economy.

There will continue to be demand for meteorologists to analyze and monitor the dispersion of pollutants into the air to ensure compliance with federal environmental regulations, but related employment increases are expected to be small. Efforts toward making and improving global weather observations also could have a positive impact on employment.

Opportunities in broadcasting are rare and highly competitive, however, making for very few job openings in this industry. Prospects for academic positions may improve. While a competitive job market will continue to exist for independent research positions in universities and for college and university faculty, opportunities are expected to be better than in the past as an increasing number of faculty are expected to retire through the projection period.

....

Salaries

Now that you know about the education you'll need and the prospects for finding a job, just how much can you earn working in the physical sciences?

Chemists

The American Chemical Society reports that in 2004 the median salary of all of its members with a bachelor's degree was $62,000; for those with a master's degree, it was $72,300; and for those with a doctorate, it was $91,600. The median annual salary was highest for those working in private industry and lowest for those in academia.

According to an American Chemical Society survey of recent graduates, inexperienced chemistry graduates with a bachelor's degree earned a median starting salary of $32,500 in October 2004; those with a master's degree earned a median salary of $43,600; and those with a doctorate had median earnings of $65,000. Among bachelor's degree graduates, those who had completed internships or had other work experience while in school commanded the highest starting salaries.

Overall, most chemists earned between $41,900 and $76,080 in 2004. Median annual earnings in the industries employing the largest numbers of chemists in May 2004 were reported as follows:

Federal government	$80,550
Scientific research and development services	$62,460
Pharmaceutical and medicine manufacturing	$57,050
Architectural, engineering, and related services	$42,370

In 2005, chemists in nonsupervisory, supervisory, and managerial positions in the federal government averaged $83,777 a year.

Physicists and Astronomers

According to a 2005 National Association of Colleges and Employers survey, the average annual starting salary offer to physics doctoral degree candidates was $56,070.

The American Institute of Physics reported a median annual salary of $104,000 in 2004 for its full-time members with doctorates (excluding those in postdoctoral positions); the median was $94,000 for those with master's degrees and $72,000 for bachelor's degree holders. Those working in temporary postdoctoral positions earned significantly less.

Overall, median annual earnings of physicists were $87,450 in May 2004. Most earned between $66,590 and $109,420; the lowest 10 percent earned less than $49,450; the highest 10 percent earned more than $132,780. The average annual salary for physicists employed by the federal government was $104,917 in 2005; for astronomy and space scientists, it was $110,195.

In May 2004, median annual earnings of astronomers were $97,320 in May 2004. Most earned between $66,190 and $120,350; the lowest 10 percent earned less than $43,410, and the highest 10 percent more than $137,860.

Geologists and Geophysicists

According to the National Association of Colleges and Employers, beginning salary offers in July 2005 for graduates with bachelor's degrees in geology and related sciences averaged $39,365 a year.

Median annual earnings of geoscientists in May 2004 were $68,730, with most earning between $49,260 and $98,380. The lowest 10 percent earned less than $37,700, and the highest 10 percent earned more than $130,750.

In 2005, the federal government's average salary for geologists in managerial, supervisory, and nonsupervisory positions was $83,178 for geologists, $94,836 for geophysicists, and $87,007 for oceanographers.

The petroleum, mineral, and mining industries are vulnerable to recessions and to changes in oil and gas prices, among other factors, and usually release workers when exploration and drilling slow down. Consequently, they offer higher salaries, but less job security, than other industries.

Meteorologists

Median annual earnings of atmospheric scientists in May 2004 were $70,100. The middle 50 percent earned between $48,880 and $86,610, while 10 percent earned less than $34,590, and 10 percent earned more than $106,020.

The average salary for meteorologists in nonsupervisory, supervisory, and managerial positions employed by the federal government was about $80,499 in 2005. Meteorologists in the federal government with a bachelor's degree and no experience received a starting salary between $27,955 and $34,544, depending on their college grades. Those with a master's degree could start between $42,090 and $54,393, and those with a doctorate could begin at $70,280. Beginning salaries for all degree levels are slightly higher in areas of the country where the prevailing local pay level is higher.

Parade of Professionals

Six scientists have shared their personal accounts. Read on to see whether one of these interesting careers might be right for you.

Sara Sawtelle, Ph.D., Chemist

Dr. Sara Sawtelle is the manager of technical services at Environmental Test Systems, Inc., in Elkhart, Indiana. ETS was founded in 1985 to develop consumer and industrial applications for reagent strip technology. Test strips have been widely used in the medical diagnostic industry since the 1960s, when their introduction revolutionized the way physicians performed urinalysis and blood tests. The company has adapted the technology for applications in such diverse fields as pool and spa water testing, drinking water quality testing, automobile and diesel truck coolant testing, and industrial in-process testing. Research and development efforts are ongoing as scientists continuously explore a variety of potential applications for the test strip.

Dr. Sawtelle earned a B.S. in science with a major in chemistry from Clarion University in Pennsylvania and a Ph.D. in analytical chemistry from Boston College. She was teaching at a local college while looking for a position that would let her use the parts of teaching that she most enjoys. ETS was seeking a chemist with good communication and people skills, and she was hired in her present position in 1997.

As manager of technical services, Dr. Sawtelle doesn't have a typical workday. She works over forty hours a week in a team-oriented atmosphere and describes her schedule as busy but not too stressful. Her position is part of the marketing department, which enables her to share her love of chemistry with others, particularly nonchemists. She assists customers with technical questions, acting as the technical liaison between the lab and the marketing department. Dr. Sawtelle talks with customers about the company's products and helps in marketing and developing new products. "I really enjoy working in this environment," she says. "The strength of this company is that from the president down to the line worker, everyone is considered important and has an invaluable function. It is a nice atmosphere in which to thrive."

Most of Dr. Sawtelle's job centers on communication—communication within the company, communication between scientists and nonscientists, and communication with customers and in presentations given to professionals in the fields that use the products. She finds her previous experience teaching chemistry at the college level to be valuable in this position, particularly in helping her to listen and not jump to conclusions about what a person may be asking.

What suggestions does Dr. Sawtelle have for aspiring chemists? "My advice is to believe in yourself and to not try to be someone else," she says. "Don't try to change who you are. And don't expect that the job you get out of college or school will be 'the job' for you. As you grow as a person, you should be willing to try new things or new career paths. I never thought I would be where I am. I expected to become a college professor. But once I tried it, I found that there were aspects of the profession that did not work for me. I like being in the position I am. So I guess my advice is to make sure you like your career—or it is just not worth your energy. If you don't like it, move on."

Ken Rubin, Ph.D., Geologist and Geophysicist

Dr. Ken Rubin serves as an associate professor on the staff of the University of Hawaii at Manoa in the department of geology and geophysics, School of Ocean and Earth Science and Technology (SOEST). He earned a B.A. in chemistry from the University of California-San Diego in 1984, followed by graduate studies at the University of California-San Diego, Scripps Institute of Oceanography, where he received his M.S. in 1985 and Ph.D. in 1991. Dr. Rubin came to the University of Hawaii in February of 1992 as an assistant researcher and became an assistant professor in January of 1995.

Dr. Rubin was hired by the University of Hawaii in a competitive search for a postdoctoral position known as the SOEST Young Investigator, which is a research faculty position (at the assistant level) that allows one to write grant proposals to federal funding agencies and to work independent of a supervisor. The positions are offered once or twice each year, and applicants are selected from a variety of disciplines, such as earth sciences, oceanography, marine biology, atmospheric sciences, and ocean engineering.

Dr. Rubin entered into an agreement with the dean and other faculty to establish a state-of-the-art thermal ionization mass spectrometry facility for analyzing radioactive isotopes. This was a significant commitment, since his position was for two years and it normally takes three to five years to fund and set up a lab of this type. However, the university agreed to extend Dr. Rubin's assistant researcher position beyond its two-year term pending significant productivity on his part. Setting up the lab required securing federal support for the purchase of a $750,000 mass spectrometer. Dr. Rubin obtained 25 percent each from the National Science Foundation Earth Sciences and Ocean Sciences Divisions and 50 percent from SOEST.

After securing the necessary funding and starting to set up the lab, Dr. Rubin was offered a position as assistant professor at the University of Miami's Rosenstiel School of Marine and Atmospheric Sciences (RSMAS). Since the economy of Hawaii was entering an economic downturn, he felt it was necessary to seek another position but hoped that the University of Hawaii would offer him a more permanent situation. In the end, an assistant professorship was approved by SOEST and the University of Hawaii. A national search was conducted to fill the position, and Dr. Rubin was selected for the job.

Although he initially wanted to be an M.D., during his freshman year of college, Dr. Rubin became very interested in chemistry with environmental applications. At the same time, he became enamored of the academic career and lifestyle, and switched his career aspirations to becoming a professor at a research university. He says, "I have nothing against private sector or government jobs and know I could find some level of fulfillment in pursuits there. However, it was clear to me then, and still is today, that the level of intellectual freedom that the university system in America affords makes this sort of job highly rewarding."

Dr. Rubin works between eight and twelve hours a day, seven days a week. One reason for this schedule is that his research requires lengthy and exacting analytical procedures that make long hours necessary. Another reason is that he enjoys his work and has taken on other duties besides research and teaching. He teaches one or two upper-division and/or graduate-level courses each semester and serves as advisor to graduate students. Dr. Rubin's lab research is done in one- to two-month intervals during which he might spend all of his time (when not teaching) in the lab, in the field, or in his office reducing data and interpreting results.

Fieldwork includes research on active volcanoes on land and on the seafloor, and almost all of the lab work involves toxic chemicals and radioactive substances. This dangerous work isn't for everyone, but Dr. Rubin finds it rewarding because of the day-to-day challenges. He says, "The part that makes it unique, and the difficult thing to pass on to students, is the application of high-precision measurements, requiring exacting care and uncompromising standards, to natural phenomena. Although the lab and fieldwork are both necessary aspects of the research we do, the two environments are very different and require different mind-sets."

In addition to teaching and research, Dr. Rubin has been involved in getting the school on the Internet. He developed and oversees numerous websites at the school, including interactive public sites providing answers to questions about science and resource sites dedicated to educating laypeople and researchers about active processes at volcanoes and the latest research going on at the University of Hawaii. "I use the Internet in my courses and love what it offers," Dr. Rubin says. "Once a person relates to and accepts the way in which people make computers process and make information available, his or her mind is freed to cross the boundaries between the abstract and the physical. Computers are a wonderful and indispensable teaching tool."

As much as he loves his work, Dr. Rubin is honest about the reality of holding an academic research position. "To enjoy the academic and intellectual freedom, friendly atmosphere, youthful environment, and flexible hours, one must be very disciplined," he says. "This can make it difficult, as you must evaluate yourself and your progress frequently and cannot rely on infrequent or nonexistent direction from a superior. You must sense the expectations of your peers and then work to satisfy them while not sacrificing your own goals and desires. You must be self-motivated and take a very long-range perspective on success in the attainment of work-related goals."

As in most academic environments, funding is an ongoing issue faced by research scientists. Dr. Rubin describes a "lack of funds at all levels. The golden age of scientific research died out in the 1980s (if not earlier). I watch my older colleagues struggling to adapt to this new environment, but since I never knew the days of seemingly unlimited research funds, I don't get as depressed as they at the difficulty of getting research funded today.

"Jobs are very difficult to obtain, so always work hard at everything you do. Not only are top-notch resumes required to land one of these jobs, but hard work will be required to keep it. A university professor's life may appear to be genteel and rewarding and filled with healthy doses of wisdom and cups of cappuccino at the local coffeehouse, but it is actually rigorous on many levels."

Kevin T. M. Johnson, Ph.D., Research Geologist

Dr. Kevin Johnson, a research geologist, is employed by both the Bishop Museum and the University of Hawaii in Honolulu. He earned a B.S. from Pennsylvania State University, an M.S. from the University of Hawaii, and a Ph.D. from MIT and the Woods Hole Oceanographic Institute in Massachusetts. He also served as a research fellow at the University of Tokyo.

Dr. Johnson has always been interested in oceans and volcanoes, which made his choice of marine geology natural. He credits his parents with introducing him to science and encouraging his academic achievements.

He describes his job as quite varied, with about 75 percent of his time spent doing basic marine geological research on projects that are funded by the National Science Foundation. The projects primarily deal with the formation of ocean basins and oceanic crust at mid-ocean ridges and oceanic islands. Dr. Johnson spends months at sea each year on research expeditions, collecting samples and data that he later analyzes on land. He also collaborates with archaeologists in studies of stone tools and secures funding from smaller agencies and contractors to carry out more specific, applied research.

In addition to his research, Dr. Johnson gives public lectures on volcanoes, geology, and earth sciences and leads field trips to Kilauea, the active volcano on the island of Hawaii. In addition, he advises museum exhibit staff on technical matters within his area of knowledge and answers questions from the public. He works between sixty and seventy hours a week and enjoys the pleasant work atmosphere and his interactions with colleagues and students.

What Dr. Johnson likes most about research is his ability to pursue questions of his own choosing and to interact with interesting and intelligent people. Since he doesn't have to punch a time clock, working in research allows him to have a lot of flexibility and a relaxed schedule.

The part that he least enjoys is the process of research proposal writing, because it is quite time-consuming and the competition for funds is very keen.

When asked what advice he would offer to other scientific types, Dr. Johnson says, "Be very studious in school and in life in general. Enjoy the world around you and be inquisitive about the natural phenomena you observe every day. Ask questions and think about possible answers."

Glen D. Lawrence, Ph.D., Biochemist

Dr. Glen Lawrence is professor of biochemistry and bioinorganic chemistry at Long Island University in Brooklyn, New York, where he has worked since 1985. He received his B.S. in chemistry from Pratt Institute in Brooklyn; his M.A. in chemistry from SUNY at

Plattsburgh, New York; and his Ph.D. in biochemistry from Utah State University in Logan, Utah. He served as a science advisor for the U.S. Food and Drug Administration New York Regional Laboratory from 1988 to 1992, advising analytical chemists in research projects related to drug chemistry.

Dr. Lawrence first became interested in the functioning of living organisms during his childhood on a farm in rural New York. Since there were no scientists in his community and he received little guidance in high school, he was not certain what direction to take after graduation. Aptitude in science and math led him to pursue a career in chemistry, and those studies brought out his fascination with biochemistry. He enrolled in a master's degree program in a chemistry department, with a biochemist as his research advisor. After completing his graduate studies, Dr. Rubin realized that he wanted to pursue a career in academia and went on to earn his doctorate in biochemistry.

With a long-standing interest in conservation, Dr. Lawrence applied for a research fellowship to study model systems for photosynthesis, wanting to study the development of materials that could be used to convert solar energy into useful chemical energy. The project was aimed at developing materials that would utilize light to catalyze the splitting of water into hydrogen and oxygen, which could later be used as fuels. Dr. Lawrence studied the problem for a year in West Germany, where he realized the difficulty of accomplishing his goal. He had the opportunity to spend several years conducting research at different laboratories, an experience that he calls extremely valuable, broadening his general knowledge of science and his specific knowledge of biochemistry, pharmacology, physiology, and toxicology.

In 1985, when funding for his research project was ending, Dr. Lawrence accepted a position at Long Island University in the master's degree program in chemistry. He says, "Although I was planning to hold out for a faculty position at a research institution, the master's degree program at the LIU Brooklyn campus provided ample opportunity for research, along with interesting possibilities for teaching advanced courses in special areas, such as neurochemistry and advanced analytical techniques for biomedical analysis."

Dr. Lawrence teaches nine hours of courses per week, including such classes as introductory chemistry for nonscience majors; chemistry for the health sciences; biochemistry for chemistry and molecular biology majors; and graduate courses in analytical chemistry, biochemistry, and neurochemistry. He occasionally teaches an elective course for honors students. In addition to teaching, Dr. Lawrence serves as advisor to undergraduate and graduate students in research projects.

Dr. Lawrence and his students work in a small lab. While their work itself is not dangerous, they nevertheless must take precautions when performing some experiments. The materials they work with are not generally explosive or toxic, but they must be aware of any that are and handle them in the proper fashion.

As a professor, Dr. Lawrence also serves on various campus committees. Though these committees vary from year to year, all take up a substantial amount of time. The committee work may include the evaluation of junior faculty members for promotion and tenure, discussion of new courses and curricula that are being proposed for the university, review of existing courses and programs and the regular reevaluation of the campus for accreditation, or attention to the day-to-day running of the university.

Dr. Lawrence is also frequently asked to review a master's degree candidate's thesis to determine whether the student meets the department's approval to obtain a degree. When he is the student's advisor, this usually requires advising the candidate about how to write a master's thesis and reading the thesis many times to make all the necessary corrections before it is submitted to the student's committee. This all occurs after guiding the student through a research project that usually lasts about a year and involves developing methods for analyzing certain chemicals, collecting a wealth of data to support a hypothesis, analyzing the data to see if it supports the hypothesis, and finally deciding how to present the data so it will be understandable to others who may be interested.

During the years that he served as science advisor to the Food and Drug Administration, Dr. Lawrence visited the FDA labs once a week to discuss research projects with the analytical chemists who analyzed drugs being sold by pharmaceutical companies. The FDA uses well-established methods for drug analysis that have undergone extensive testing in both the FDA labs and the pharmaceutical manufacturers' labs. Some of these methods rely on procedures that may be many years old; in some cases, newer methods could save much time without sacrificing accuracy. However, any new method must be tested before it can become an established method in their protocol.

Dr. Lawrence's job was to work with the FDA chemists in an attempt to streamline the methods used to accomplish efficient and accurate drug analysis. An example of this involved an analysis for the Department of Defense of the drugs in nerve gas antidotes. When the Persian Gulf War began, nerve gas antidotes had to be taken from storage and tested quickly to determine their suitability for use, since much of the stockpile had passed the expiration date. The existing method required forty-five minutes per sample for testing. Dr. Lawrence tried a different method that decreased the analysis time to ten minutes, which is a significant savings in time when thousands of samples must be tested. Once the new method was thoroughly tested, it was found to be very suitable for military samples as well as for a wide variety of dosage forms, including eye drops and some other medications.

Dr. Lawrence finds a lot of satisfaction in his career. He says, "Whether in the classroom or the laboratory, teaching can be very exciting. Other times it can be extremely frustrating. Sometimes students show a genuine interest in the material; other times I get a whole classroom of students who just don't want to be there (but it is a requirement for them to graduate). Many come into the class dreading it initially but find after a while that we are covering things that can be quite interesting, such as the greenhouse effect, global warming, air and water pollution, destruction of the ozone layer, and guidelines about how to keep your body healthy. By the time the students get finished, some of them realize that it was a worthwhile college experience.

"Probably the most rewarding aspect of my job is realized when a student decides to do a special project, either in the form of research in the lab or a library research project, and that student begins to comprehend the complexities of science, especially the life sciences. If I feel that I can instill in another individual the desire to pursue a career in science or just to understand more about how the world works on the molecular level, then I feel I have accomplished my goal. Even if only a handful of my students realize this in my lifetime, I will have passed something on to the next generation."

Charles L. Dumoulin, Ph.D., Research Physicist

Dr. Charles Dumoulin, a research scientist, serves as a physicist in the field of medicine. He has been on staff at General Electric's Research and Development Center in Schenectady, New York, since 1984. In 1996, he received the center's highest honor, its Coolidge Fellowship Award, which recognizes sustained contribution to science or engineering. Dr. Dumoulin was honored for his pioneering contributions to magnetic resonance imaging (MRI). He has published eighty-three peer-reviewed papers and twenty-four chapters in books, and he has had sixty-one issued patents and currently has eleven patents pending. In 2005, he received a gold medal award from the International Society for Magnetic Resonance in Medicine.

Although he was always fascinated by science and had a knack for science and math, Dr. Dumoulin's original career plan was to become a military officer. When he learned that his eyesight was too poor, he changed his plans and went to Florida State University, choosing chemistry as his major. After school and during summer vacations, he worked in a television and appliance repair shop, where he realized that he enjoyed learning how things work. He also learned that the best way to understand something was to take it apart, fix it, and put it back together. He found solving problems enjoyable. Once he became a researcher, he found that the most exciting problems to tackle were those that required creative solutions and addressed real-life problems, and that unlike many fields, science generally dealt with questions that have objective and provable answers.

Subsequently, Dr. Dumoulin earned a Ph.D. from Florida State University in analytical chemistry. He followed his thesis professor to Syracuse University, where he became a nontenure-track assistant professor. For three years he helped run a lab, conducted research, and cofounded a small company but eventually realized that this environment was not allowing him to develop as a researcher. He moved to GE's Research and Development Center, where he changed his focus from nuclear magnetic resonance spectroscopy for chemistry to the related topic of magnetic resonance (MR) for medical applications.

In his present position, Dr. Dumoulin works as a physicist in the field of medicine, with the primary goal of developing new ways to perform diagnostic and interventional procedures with magnetic resonance imaging (MRI) scanners. His major projects have included MR spectroscopy, MR angiography (use of radio frequency signals to follow devices in real time), MR measurements of kidney function, MR tracking of interventional devices in real time, cardiac MR imaging, and use of MR to increase basic understanding of flow physiology in blood vessels.

Although his scheduled workweek is forty hours, he typically works eight to nine hours a day and often a few hours during the weekend. Dr. Dumoulin says that he often finds himself thinking about work-related problems and finds that some of his most productive moments occur while trying to sleep and driving to or from work.

Since he works in industry, Dr. Dumoulin's job is somewhat different from that of an academic scientist working in a university. For example, he must justify his work as having some relevance to the company, which means that most of what he does can be called applied science rather than basic science.

Dr. Dumoulin describes the work atmosphere at GE as relatively relaxed, but with an intensity of purpose. His colleagues have been trained in a number of different scientific disciplines (such as computer science, physical chemistry, physics, astrophysics, medicine, electrical engineering). They work in ad hoc teams, and conflicts are rare. He enjoys the fact that every day brings unique challenges and tasks. A typical day begins with reading and answering e-mail. One or two days a week he uses the MRI scanner to test new ideas and perform experiments. When he's not in the lab, he is usually at his desk writing (e-mail, memos, papers, and so on) or in meetings with his colleagues.

Dr. Dumoulin's job requires frequent travel. He attends conferences, where he speaks about his work and learns about other scientists' projects, which he finds inspiring. He also visits research hospitals around the world, where he works with doctors to develop and evaluate new ways of using MRI scanners.

Dr. Dumoulin finds the best parts of his career to be the intellectual challenge of finding creative solutions to problems, the exposure to new ideas within and beyond his profession, and working on medical diagnostic methods that have direct relevance to patients. He also enjoys having the latitude to define his own research agenda, working with some of the best scientists and engineers in the world, and the opportunity to talk to students of all ages about science and technology.

The more negative aspects of his career include those things that get in the way of productivity and the difficulty of securing funding for projects and patent protection for all of his inventions. In addition, there is a lack of tenure in the industry, and compensation for scientists is not commensurate with their contributions to society. There is also a lack of wide-ranging opportunities for people in Dr. Dumoulin's specialty.

"I would recommend to all prospective scientists that you remain as broad as possible," Dr. Dumoulin says. "Scientific success often occurs by the synergistic combination of two or more existing ideas from different disciplines. It's important to stay focused on completing projects. But somehow you must concentrate on each project at every stage of its being. And usually a project is not considered complete until a publication (a memo, paper, or patent application, for example) is submitted.

"It is always in your best interests to use the golden rule when dealing with everyone. Be particularly sensitive to the issue of sharing credit with your coworkers. Virtually all discoveries are accomplished as a result of the efforts of many—be sure everyone gets their just portion of the rewards!"

Eric S. Posmentier, Ph.D., Geophysicist

Dr. Eric Posmentier is professor of physics and mathematics at the Brooklyn Campus of Long Island University, New York. He earned a B.S. in physics from the City College of New York and a Ph.D. in geophysics from Columbia University.

At a time when global warming was still viewed with skepticism by many scientists, Dr. Posmentier and his colleagues at Columbia University used data from the tropical Pacific Ocean to publish evidence that global warming had begun.

Dr. Posmentier is currently working with a group of scientists at the Harvard/Smithsonian Astrophysical Observatory. They are studying variations of the brightness of the sun, and he has published peer-reviewed papers on climate.

Dr. Posmentier has been fascinated by nature and curious about explanations of natural phenomena ever since elementary school.

He was drawn to any kind of scientific activity, such as collecting rocks, dissecting a dead bird, or experimenting with a chemistry set. By high school, he knew that he wanted a career in the physical sciences or mathematics, and he discovered in college that geophysical sciences (physics of the atmosphere, oceans, and solid earth) held the greatest attraction for him., He has since added quantum mechanics to his active research.

Dr. Posmentier attributes the development of his interests to teachers and professors who gave him self-confidence and who shared their excitement of discovering knowledge, skills, and concepts. He cites two particularly formative experiences from high school and college. One was a Bronx High School of Science sophomore course devoted to individual biology research projects, where he learned how challenging it is to design an original experiment and how rewarding it is to succeed. The other experience was the opportunity to work part-time (while still in college) with graduate students and Ph.D.s in a research laboratory at Columbia University. There he discovered how satisfying it can be to apply the concepts and skills he was still acquiring to unsolved problems, making some progress and uncovering still new questions.

While in college, Dr. Posmentier realized that geophysics combined several of his greatest passions: studying our planet, applying the disciplines of physics and mathematics, and spending time outdoors observing. He is especially attracted to problems that cross specializations, such as the physics of global warming and the economics of energy use, or ocean currents and the fishing industry, or seismic detection of earthquakes and explosions and the politics of disarmament. As a professor, he also enjoys sharing his knowledge of and excitement for science with the next generation.

On most days, Dr. Posmentier works in his office for up to eleven hours. He spends about half of his time preparing for classes, lecturing, meeting with students, writing, grading exams, and meeting with other professors to discuss academic matters. The rest of the time is spent reading and conducting research.

Although most of his research time is spent sitting at a desk or in front of a computer, Dr. Posmentier has occasionally traveled to the mountains to observe air and clouds or rocks and forests, and he has taken boats out to scuba dive in rivers, lakes, bays, estuaries, and the ocean in order to observe the water and its movement.

Since he is usually involved in several things at once, a typical day is busy and hectic, but there are always times when he can change the pace by having informal discussions with colleagues about work. The ideas that come out of these informal discussions are frequently as important, in their own way, as the results of the long, disciplined hours spent alone writing, deriving mathematics, or computing. When he is deeply engrossed in a research problem, he often works on it in the evenings and on weekends.

Regarding what he likes most and least about his job, Dr. Posmentier says, "I experience the very best part of this work at the moment a new concept is discovered and the instant my students catch on to a concept I am teaching. Least favorite is grading, grading, grading."

Dr. Posmentier has the following suggestions to offer aspiring scientists: "I would advise that you emphasize the fundamental sciences and mathematics in your courses," he says. "You should study interdisciplinary applications, such as environmental science or marine science only in addition to—never instead of—physics, chemistry, biology, and mathematics. The latter are the foundation upon which all the rest will have to stand. Find a teacher or professor who is willing to guide you in formulating and working on an individual research problem for a week, a year, or a lifetime."

For More Information

General information on career opportunities and earnings for chemists is available from:

American Chemical Society
1155 Sixteenth Street NW
Washington, DC 20036
www.chemistry.org

Chemical Institute of Canada
130 Rue Slater Street, Suite 550
Ottawa, ON K1P 6E2
Canada
www.cheminst.ca

For general information on opportunities in physics, contact:

American Institute of Physics
One Physics Ellipse
College Park, MD 20740
www.aip.org

The American Physical Society
One Physics Ellipse
College Park, MD 20740
www.aps.org

Canadian Association of Physicists
MacDonald Building, Suite 112
150 Louis Pasteur Priv.
Ottawa, ON K1N 6N5
Canada
www.cap.ca

Information on careers in astronomy is available from:

American Astronomical Society
2000 Florida Avenue NW, Suite 400
Washington, DC 20009
www.aas.org

Canadian Astronomical Society
Department of Physics
Queens University
Kingston, ON K7L 3N6
Canada
www.casca.ca

Information on opportunities for geologists is available from:

American Geological Institute
4220 King Street
Alexandria, VA 22302
www.agiweb.org

Geological Association of Canada
Department of Earth Sciences
Room ER4063, Alexander Murray Building
Memorial University of Newfoundland
St. John's, NL A1B 3X5
Canada
www.gac.ca

Geological Society of America
PO Box 9140
Boulder, CO 80301
www.geosociety.org

American Association of Petroleum Geologists
1444 South Boulder
Tulsa, OK 74119
www.aapg.org

Canadian Society of Petroleum Geologists
600, 640 Eighth Avenue SW
Calgary, AL T2P 1G7
Canada
www.cspg.org

Information on training and career opportunities for geophysicists is available from:

American Geophysical Union
2000 Florida Avenue NW
Washington, DC 20009
www.agu.org

Canadian Geophysical Union
Department of Geology & Geophysics
University of Calgary
ES 278, 2500 University Drive NW
Calgary, AL T2N 1N4
Canada
www.cgu-ugc.ca

A list of education and training programs in oceanography and related fields is available from:

Marine Technology Society
5565 Sterrett Place, Suite 108
Columbia, MD 20144
www.mtsociety.org

Information on career opportunities in meteorology is available from:

American Meteorological Society
45 Beacon Street
Boston, MA 02108
www.ametsoc.org

Canadian Meteorological and Oceanographic Society
PO Box 3211
Station D
Ottawa, ON K1P 6H7
Canada
www.cmos.ca

Information on acquiring a job as a chemist, physicist, astronomer, geologist, geophysicist, or meteorologist with the federal government may be obtained from the Office of Personnel Management (OPM). Visit the website at www.usajobs.com. In Canada, visit www.jobs-emplois.gc.ca for federal job postings.

CHAPTER FOUR

Careers in the Agricultural Sciences

The whole of science is nothing more than a refinement of everyday thinking.
—Albert Einstein

Can you think of anything more important than food? It is at the very core of our existence. Food technology incorporates the application of science to the commercial processing of foodstuffs. Foods are processed to make them more palatable or digestible; to prevent the growth of bacteria, molds, yeasts, and other microorganisms; or to preserve them from spoiling—a process caused by the action of enzymes within the food that changes its chemical composition, resulting in changes in flavor, odor, color, and texture. For instance, preservation enables foods that are seasonally produced to be available all year. Such is the work of agricultural scientists.

Agricultural Scientists

The work of agricultural scientists plays an important part in maintaining and increasing the nation's agricultural productivity. These scientists study farm crops and animals and develop ways of improving their quantity and quality. They look for ways to improve crop yield and quality with less labor, avenues to control pests and weeds more safely and effectively, and techniques to conserve soil and water. They research methods of converting raw agricultural commodities into attractive and healthy food products for consumers.

Agricultural science is closely related to biological science, because it uses the principles of biology, chemistry, and other sciences to solve problems in agriculture. Scientists from both disciplines often work together on basic biological research, or they may concentrate on applying the technological advances to agriculture.

In the past two decades, rapid advances in basic biological knowledge related to genetics have spurred growth in the field of biotechnology. Some agricultural scientists use this technology to manipulate the genetic material of plants and crops, attempting to make organisms more productive or resistant to disease. These advances in biotechnology have opened up research opportunities in many areas of agricultural science, including commercial applications in agriculture, environmental remediation, and the food industry. Another emerging technology expected to affect agriculture is nanotechnology, a future molecular manufacturing technology that promises to revolutionize methods of manufacturing and distribution in many industries.

Many agricultural scientists work in basic or applied research and development. Others manage or administer research and development programs or manage marketing or production operations in companies that produce food products or agricultural chemicals, supplies, and machinery. Some are consultants to business firms, private clients, or government. Depending on the agricultural scientist's area of specialization, the nature of the work performed varies.

Food Science

Food scientists or food technologists are usually employed in the food processing industry, at universities, or by the federal government. They help meet consumer demand for food products that are healthful, safe, palatable, and convenient. To accomplish this, they use their knowledge of chemistry, microbiology, and other sciences to develop new or better ways of preserving, processing, packaging, storing, and delivering foods.

Some food scientists engage in basic research, working on projects involving the discovery of new food sources; the analysis of food content to determine levels of vitamins, fat, sugar, or protein; or the search for potential substitutes for harmful or undesirable food additives, such as nitrites. Many food technologists work in product development. Others enforce government regulations, inspecting food processing areas and ensuring that sanitation, safety, quality, and waste management standards are met.

Plant Science

Plant science includes the disciplines of agronomy, crop science, entomology, and plant breeding, among others. Scientists in these areas study plants and their growth in soils, helping producers of food, feed, and fiber crops continue to feed a growing population while conserving natural resources and maintaining the environment. Agronomists and crop scientists not only help increase productivity but also study ways to improve the nutritional value of crops and the quality of seed. Some crop scientists study the breeding, physiology, and management of crops and use genetic engineering to develop crops resistant to pests and drought.

Soil Science

Soil scientists explore the chemical, physical, biological, and mineralogical composition of soils as they relate to plant or crop growth. They study the responses of various soil types to fertilizers, tillage practices, and crop rotation. Many soil scientists who work for the federal government conduct soil surveys, classifying and mapping soils. They provide information and recommendations to farmers and other landowners regarding the best use of land and how to avoid or correct problems such as erosion. They may also consult with engineers and other technical personnel working on construction projects about the effects of—and solutions to—soil problems. Because soil science is closely related to environmental science, people trained in soil science also apply their knowledge to ensure environmental quality and effective land use.

Animal Science

Animal scientists develop better, more efficient ways of producing and processing meat, poultry, eggs, and milk. Dairy scientists, poultry scientists, animal breeders, and other related scientists study the genetics, nutrition, reproduction, growth, and development of domestic farm animals. Some animal scientists inspect and grade livestock or other food products, purchase livestock, or work in technical sales or marketing. As extension agents or consultants, animal scientists advise agricultural producers on how to upgrade animal housing facilities properly, lower mortality rates, or increase production of animal products such as milk or eggs. Entomologists may talk to local farmers about insect problems in growing corn and other crops.

Education and Training

The training that you'll need to work as an agricultural scientist will depend on the area you plan to specialize in and the type of work you'll perform. A bachelor's degree in agricultural science is sufficient for some jobs in applied research or for assisting in basic research, but you need a master's or doctoral degree to work in basic research.

A doctorate in agricultural science usually is needed for college teaching and for advancement to administrative research positions. Degrees in related sciences such as biology, chemistry, or physics or in related engineering specialties also may qualify you for some agricultural science jobs.

You can find agricultural science programs at every state land-grant college, as well as many other colleges and universities. A typical undergraduate agricultural science curriculum includes communications, mathematics, economics, business, and physical and life sciences courses, in addition to a wide variety of technical agricultural science courses. If you are interested in animal science, your program might also include animal breeding, reproductive physiology, nutrition, and meats and muscle biology.

If you pursue graduate studies, you'd typically specialize in a subfield of agricultural science, such as animal breeding and genetics, crop science, or horticulture science, depending on your interest and the kind of work you wish to do. For example, if you're interested in doing genetic and biotechnological research in the food industry, you need to develop a strong background in life and physical sciences, such as cell and molecular biology, microbiology, and inorganic and organic chemistry.

You normally won't need to specialize at the undergraduate level. In fact, undergraduates who are broadly trained have greater flexibility when changing jobs than if they had narrowly defined their interests.

To prepare for a career as a food scientist, take courses in food chemistry, food analysis, food microbiology, food engineering, and food processing operations. If you study crop or soil science, your program will include classes in plant pathology, soil chemistry, entomology, plant physiology, and biochemistry, among others. Advanced degree programs include classroom and fieldwork, laboratory research, and a thesis or dissertation based on independent research.

To be successful as an agricultural or food scientist, you should be able to work independently or as part of a team and be able to communicate clearly and concisely, both orally and in writing. You should also have an understanding of basic business principles and the ability to apply basic statistical techniques. Employers increasingly prefer job applicants who are able to apply computer skills to determine solutions to problems, to collect and analyze data, and to control various processes.

The American Society of Agronomy offers certification programs in crop science, agronomy, crop advising, soil science, plant pathology, and weed science. To become certified, you must pass designated examinations and have a minimum of two years of experience with at least a bachelor's degree in agriculture or four years of experience with no degree. You don't need a degree to become a certified crop advisor, however.

With an advanced degree, your career will likely begin in research or teaching. With experience, you may advance to jobs such as supervisor of research programs or manager of other agriculture-related activities.

Job Outlook

Employment of agricultural and food scientists is expected to grow between 9 and 17 percent through 2014. Past agricultural research has resulted in the development of higher-yielding crops, crops with better resistance to pests and plant pathogens, and chemically based fertilizers and pesticides. Research is still necessary—particularly as insects and diseases continue to adapt to pesticides and as soil fertility and water quality continue to need improvement—resulting in job opportunities in biotechnology. Agricultural scientists are using new avenues of research in biotechnology to develop plants and food crops that require less fertilizer, fewer pesticides and herbicides, and even less water for growth. Emerging biotechnologies and nanotechnologies will play an increasingly larger role in creating more plentiful global food supplies.

Biotechnological research will continue to offer possibilities for the development of new food products. This research will allow agricultural and food scientists to develop techniques to detect and control food pathogens and should lead to better understanding of other infectious agents in foods.

Agricultural scientists will be needed to balance increased agricultural output with protection and preservation of soil, water, and ecosystems. They will increasingly encourage the practice of sustainable agriculture by developing and implementing plans to manage pests, crops, soil fertility and erosion, and animal waste in ways that reduce the use of harmful chemicals and do minimal damage to farms and the natural environment.

Further studies at scientific research and development services firms should result in more job opportunities. This research will be stimulated by a heightened public focus on diet, health, changes in food safety, and biosecurity—preventing the introduction of infectious agents, such as foot-and-mouth disease, into a herd of animals. Increasing demand for these workers also will stem from issues such as a growing world population; availability and cost of usable water; shrinking natural resources, including the loss of arable land; and deforestation, environmental pollution, and climate change.

Graduates with a bachelor's degree should find work in a variety of fields related to agriculture and food science, mostly in the private sector. A bachelor's degree in agricultural science is useful for managerial jobs in businesses that deal with ranchers and farmers, such as feed, fertilizer, seed, and farm equipment manufacturers; retailers or wholesalers; and farm credit institutions.

In some cases, those with a four-year degree can provide consulting services or work in sales and marketing, promoting high-demand products such as organic foods. Bachelor's degree holders also can work in some applied research and product development positions under the guidance of a scientist with a doctorate, but usually only in certain subfields, such as food science and technology. The federal government hires bachelor's degree holders to work as soil scientists. Four-year degrees can also be helpful for entering occupations such as farmer, farm or ranch manager, cooperative extension service agent, agricultural products inspector, or purchasing or sales agent for agricultural commodity or farm supply companies.

Opportunities may be better for those with a master's degree, particularly for graduates seeking applied research positions in a laboratory. Master's degree candidates also can seek to become a certified crop advisor, helping farmers better manage their crops. Those with a doctorate in agricultural and food science will experience the best opportunities, especially in basic research and teaching positions at colleges and universities because retirements of faculty are expected to accelerate during the projection period.

Fewer opportunities for agricultural and food scientists are expected in the federal government, mostly because of budgetary cutbacks at the U.S. Department of Agriculture.

Employment of agricultural and food scientists is relatively stable during periods of economic recession. Layoffs are less likely among agricultural and food scientists than in some other occupations because food is a staple item and its demand fluctuates very little with economic activity.

Salaries

According to the National Association of Colleges and Employers, beginning salary offers in 2005 for graduates with a bachelor's degree in animal sciences averaged $30,614 a year; plant sciences, $31,649 a year; and in other agricultural sciences, $36,189 a year.

Overall, median annual earnings of food scientists and technologists were $50,840 in May 2004. The majority earned between $36,450 and $72,510; ten percent earned less than $28,410, and 10 percent earned more than $91,300.

Median annual earnings of soil and plant scientists were $51,200 in May 2004, with most earning between $37,890 and $69,120. The lowest 10 percent earned less than $30,660, and the highest 10 percent earned more than $88,840. Median annual earnings of animal scientists were $49,920.

The average federal salary for employees in nonsupervisory, supervisory, and managerial positions in 2005 was $87,025 in animal science and $73,573 in agronomy.

Parade of Professionals

If you think you'd like to pursue a career in agricultural science, read the following accounts to see whether any of these professionals' experiences intrigue you.

Carl I. Evensen, Ph.D., Agronomist

Dr. Evensen is chair of the Department of Natural Resources and Environmental Management at the University of Hawaii in Honolulu, where he has also served as assistant extension specialist for natural resource management and environmental quality in the Department of Agronomy and Soil Science. He has a B.S. in biology from Whitman College in Walla Walla, Washington, and an M.S. and Ph.D. in agronomy and soil science from the University of Hawaii at Manoa.

Dr. Evensen felt that his decision to pursue agriculture as a profession was a natural one, because he has always enjoyed gardening and growing crops. He also likes working with other people and has found that he truly enjoys agricultural extension work because it combines his interests and inclinations.

After earning his bachelor's degree, Dr. Evensen was still uncertain about which profession to pursue. He decided to take some time to think about his future and try to give something back to society, so he joined the Peace Corps. He spent two years working in an isolated part of Kenya as a horticultural extensionist. He describes that as a life-changing experience that reinforced his desire to work in agriculture, pointed out the gaps in his knowledge, and convinced him attend the tropical agricultural program at the University of Hawaii.

Dr. Evensen spent his master's program studying agroforestry in Hawaii and conducted his doctoral research in Indonesia, working on a soil management project. These studies gave him a strong background in soil fertility and crop nutrition and helped him understand the needs of foreign graduate students. He was an agronomist at the Hawaii Sugar Planters' Association, where he gained valuable experience with large-scale plantation agriculture, as well as working with soil and water conservation issues and problems.

Dr. Evensen offers some advice for aspiring scientists. "I feel this type of job is very rewarding but also overwhelming and all-consuming," he says. "It is important to be organized and frequently reprioritize the multiple and changing activities so that the really critical things get done in a timely manner. However, it is also very important to avoid becoming consumed by the job. You must make time for yourself and your family because there is a danger of becoming burned out."

Michael Moore, Ph.D., Taxonomist

Dr. Michael Moore, a taxonomist, is curator of the Plant Department at the University of Georgia, where he studied as an undergraduate. He stayed on as a graduate student and earned his master's and doctorate as well. He was fortunate enough to get a job at the university even before he finished school and has been curator of the herbarium (plant museum) for nine years.

Most major universities have herbaria, and the number of curators they employ will depend on how many specimens they house. For example, a very large herbarium will have individual curators who are responsible for certain species or categories of plants. The herbarium at the University of Georgia is the largest in the state, with over two hundred thousand specimens. As curator, Dr. Moore is responsible for making sure that the collection is properly maintained and curated. He also has research projects that take him into the field, and he enjoys this ability to work both indoors and outdoors.

In addition to his other responsibilities, Dr. Moore responds to questions from the public. He also arranges the exchange of specimens and loan of plants with other herbaria and handles plant identifications. He has also taught some classes at the university.

Dr. Moore points out that taxonomists may be called upon to do many things, and the proper education is a necessity for success. He says, "It's important to realize that a master's degree is usually a requirement and a doctorate is preferred for those who wish to embark upon this career. If you wish to focus on academia, you can do research as well as teach. Then you would want a heavy background in molecular biology and similar course work. If you want to be more of a field botanist—that is, someone who does more or less what I do in herbaria—or work with a private company protecting endangered species, you would want to have more ornamental horticulture training.

"There are a number of hot topics that require the services of professionals in this field: conservation of the rain forest and environmental issues, for example. In the future, I think there will still be jobs for those who have a good basic background in taxonomy and are able to do basic field research."

Art Davis, Ph.D., Cereal Chemist

Dr. Art Davis, a cereal chemist, is the director of scientific services at the American Association of Cereal Chemists. He earned his bachelor's degree from Oregon State University, then spent two years in the Peace Corps. He earned his master's degree and doctorate in cereal chemistry from Kansas State University.

Dr. Davis worked in the research and development department at the Pillsbury Company, and then headed a research group for the American Institute of Baking. Following that, he served on the faculty of Kansas State University for nine years, then he worked in positions as quality assurance manager for General Foods Bakeries and director of technical services for the Green Giant Fresh Vegetables Group.

One of the main functions of the American Association of Cereal Chemists is education. The AACC offers about thirty short courses and other continuing education programs. It tries to provide basic information in food science wherever it sees a need. For example, when the use of frozen foods grew rapidly several years ago, the AACC provided training for smaller companies that were interested in entering the field. The association found people who were knowledgeable about the topic and put together a two-day course that provided the basics for those who needed the information.

Other AACC courses include water activity, wet milling sensory analysis, food technology, batter and breading technology, chemical leavening, breakfast cereal technology, chemistry technology, and principles of cereal science. The AACC is often contacted by people with backgrounds in biology, microbiology, or engineering who have no food experience, and its courses provide the information needed.

Another service provided by the AACC is an international check sample service. Samples are sent to participating laboratories that perform specific analyses. The results are sent to the AACC, which compiles all of the results and provides a report that reveals the status of perhaps a hundred laboratories. This gives the labs some idea of whether or not they are in line with other labs and how accurate their findings are. The AACC also does proficiency certification—if a lab sends all of its samples in for a year and the results are consistent with other labs, the AACC will issue a certificate verifying that fact.

Dr. Davis points out that because there's a critical size that must be reached before it's feasible to establish your own research and development group, smaller companies tend to depend on their suppliers to do their research and development for them. For instance, his experience at the General Foods Bakeries taught him that you can mix doughnut batter—starting with flour, sugar, salt, and so forth—without a problem. However, because of some of the peculiarities of putting doughnut mixes together, it's a lot more efficient to buy a mix from a company that makes doughnut mixes. If there's a problem with the mix, the customer can ask the company to solve it or to create something different.

Dr. Davis has some very specific advice for prospective food scientists. He says, "For those interested in getting into food science, I would highly recommend Kansas State University's Department of Grain Science and Industry. They've got three curricula there: milling, baking, and seed plants (which has to do with building animal feeds). The undergraduate program, which includes serious chemistry, physics, and a little bit of engineering, is so excellent that every student who graduates from there has at least a couple of job offers. There is also a graduate program, and they never have any trouble placing those people either.

"Minnesota has a small but growing program in the cereals area through their food science department. Iowa State and Texas A&M do some good work. At the graduate level, Kansas State and North Dakota State University have good graduate programs, and Texas A&M has a graduate group that works in cereals, as does Iowa State. Just drop a line to those universities and see if their programs are of interest to you.

"If you are planning on doing research at a university, I'd recommend that you get a Ph.D. However, industry doesn't get terribly hung up on degrees. I know a number of good researchers with master's degrees who have gone on and done quite well. I even know of a few with bachelor's degrees who have distinguished themselves. If you are an able researcher, there are opportunities out there for you."

Brent Steven Sipes, Ph.D., Plant Pathologist

Dr. Brent Sipes is associate plant pathologist and graduate chair for tropical plant pathology at the University of Hawaii's Department of Plant Pathology in Honolulu. He came to the university as a junior researcher in 1991 to evaluate pineapple for resistance or tolerance to a plant parasite. He earned his B.S. in plant pathology from Purdue University in West Lafayette, Indiana, and went on to earn his M.S. and Ph.D. in the same field from North Carolina State University in Raleigh.

Dr. Sipes has always enjoyed the outdoors and plants, and as a child he was encouraged to garden by a neighbor. He has been interested in plants and their biology, systematics, and cultivation ever since. He is also very conscientious about environmental issues, and this activism motivated him to help in the proper use of pesticides. Becoming a plant pathologist was a natural outgrowth of these interests.

His first job was in a commercial greenhouse in Louisville, Kentucky. The company grew roses that were shipped throughout the Midwest. Dr. Sipes also spent three college summers working at the Morton Arboretum in a suburb of Chicago. He was tutored by professional horticulturists who cared about plants and their well-being and who instilled in him the desire to perform quality work that would ensure that future generations would enjoy the plants in the arboretum's collections.

Dr. Sipes did well in college and knew before graduation that he would pursue an advanced degree. In graduate school he learned that he enjoyed the thrill of collecting and analyzing data from experiments and of formulating and asking questions, as well as conducting research.

In his present position, the daily schedule can vary greatly. Some days are spent indoors attending committee meetings; others are spent at his desk analyzing and preparing data for presentations. The days that Dr. Sipes enjoys most are those that he spends outside in the field collecting samples, setting up a test, or treating an experiment. Sometimes he is asked to travel to experiments on neighboring islands, and he attends scientific meetings all over the world.

Dr. Sipes is at liberty to structure his days as he see fit. He likes to start early, while the day is cool (around 7 A.M.), and finish before it gets very hot (by about 4 P.M.), even if he is working inside all day. Because 60 percent of his work involves field experiments, much of its completion depends on the weather. Consequently, the work is sometimes very slow and easy, while at other times it seems that too much needs to be done in the allotted time. He works about fifty hours a week but enjoys the job enough that he doesn't keep track of the hours.

The job requires him to work with many different types of people, from senior professors and administrators to technical staff who assist students with research. Each group is different and the challenge is to work well with everyone. He describes the people in his lab as similar to a family who all get along well together.

What Dr. Sipes likes most about his work is the ability to pose questions and contemplate how to answer them. He least likes having to analyze the data in order to answer those questions. Overall, he is honored by the respect his work affords him in the community.

"If you are interested and excited by this career, then commit yourself to it," Dr. Sipes says. "The most important aspect to living is to enjoy your livelihood. Do not work to live on the weekends."

For More Information

Information on careers in agricultural science is available from:

Agricultural Institute of Canada
280 Albert Street, Suite 900
Ottawa, ON K1P 5G8
Canada
www.aic.ca

American Society of Agronomy
677 South Segoe Road
Madison, WI 53711
www.agronomy.org

Canadian Society of Agronomy
PO Box 637
Pinawa, MB R0E 1L0
Canada
www.agronomycanada.com

Canadian Society of Soil Science
PO Box 637
Pinawa, MB R0E 1L0
Canada
www.csss.ca

Crop Science Society of America
677 South Segoe Road
Madison, WI 53711
www.crops.org

Soil Science Society of America
677 South Segoe Road
Madison, WI 53711
www.soils.org

For information on career opportunities in food technology, contact:

Institute of Food Technologists
525 West Van Buren, Suite 1000
Chicago, IL 60607
www.ift.org

For information on careers in entomology, contact:

Entomological Society of America
10001 Derekwood Lane, Suite 100
Lanham, MD 20706
www.entsoc.org

Entomological Society of Canada
393 Winston Avenue
Ottawa, ON K2A 1Y8
Canada
www.esc-sec.org

Information on acquiring a job as an agricultural scientist with the federal government may be obtained from the Office of Personnel Management. Visit the website at www.usajobs.com. In Canada, visit www.jobs-emplois.gc.ca for federal job postings.

CHAPTER FIVE

Careers in Engineering

The outcome of any serious research can only be to make two questions grow where one question grew before.
—Thorstein Veblen

Historic engineering feats during the twentieth century include the Panama Canal in 1914; the Empire State Building, television, and the electron microscope in 1931; the Golden Gate Bridge in 1937; nuclear power in the 1950s; lasers in 1956; the microprocessor in 1958; the artificial heart in 1967; jumbo jets and the Apollo moon landing in 1969; the procedure known as the CAT scan in the 1970s; fiber-optic communications and the trans-Alaska pipeline in 1977; and computer-aided design in the 1970s. All of these incredible advances were the result of intense effort on the part of countless engineers who endeavored to develop new and improved products, technological advances, and healthier and more prosperous ways to live.

Engineers

Engineers apply the theories and principles of science and mathematics to the economical solution of practical technical problems. Their work is often the link between a scientific discovery and its commercial application.

It is the responsibility of engineers to create machinery, products, systems, and processes for efficient and economical performance. They design industrial machinery and equipment for manufacturing defense-related goods and weapons systems for the armed forces in addition to designing, planning, and supervising the construction of buildings, highways, and rapid transit systems. They also design and develop systems for control and automation of manufacturing, business, and management.

Engineers consider many factors in developing new products. For example, to develop an industrial robot, they determine precisely what function it needs to perform; design and test the necessary components; fit them together in an integrated plan; and evaluate the design's overall effectiveness, cost, reliability, and safety. This process applies to products as different as chemicals, computers, gas turbines, helicopters, and toys.

In addition to design and development, many engineers work in testing, production, or maintenance. They supervise production in factories, determine the causes of breakdowns, and test manufactured products to maintain quality. They also estimate the time and cost to complete projects. Some work in engineering management or in sales, where an engineering background enables them to discuss the technical aspects of a product and assist in planning its installation or use.

Engineers use computers to simulate and test how a machine, structure, or system operates. They also use computer-aided design to produce and analyze designs. They write reports and consult with other engineers, as complex projects often require an interdisciplinary team of engineers. Supervisory engineers are responsible for major components or entire projects.

Engineering Specialties

Most engineers choose to specialize in a particular area. More than twenty-five major specialties are recognized by professional societies, and within the major branches are numerous subdivisions. Structural, environmental, and transportation engineering, for example, are subdivisions of civil engineering. Engineers also may specialize in one industry, such as motor vehicles, or in one field of technology, such as propulsion or guidance systems.

Aerospace Engineers

Aerospace engineers design, develop, test, and help manufacture commercial and military aircraft, missiles, and spacecraft. They develop new technologies for use in commercial aviation, defense systems, and space exploration, often specializing in areas such as structural design, guidance, navigation and control, instrumentation and communication, or production methods.

They also may specialize in a particular type of aerospace product, such as commercial transports, helicopters, spacecraft, or rockets. Aerospace engineers may be experts in aerodynamics, propulsion, thermodynamics, structures, celestial mechanics, acoustics, or guidance and control systems.

Chemical Engineers

Chemical engineers apply the principles of chemistry and engineering to solve problems involving the production or use of chemicals. Most work in the production of chemicals and chemical products.

Chemical engineers design equipment and develop processes for manufacturing chemicals, plan and test methods of manufacturing the products, and supervise production. They also work in industries other than chemical manufacturing, such as electronics or aircraft manufacturing.

Because the knowledge and duties of chemical engineers cut across many fields, they apply principles of chemistry, physics, mathematics, and mechanical and electrical engineering in their work. They frequently specialize in a particular operation, such as oxidation or polymerization. Other chemical engineers choose to specialize in a particular area, such as pollution control or the production of a specific product like automotive plastics or chlorine bleach.

Civil Engineers

Civil engineers work in the oldest branch of engineering. They design and supervise the construction of roads, airports, tunnels, bridges, water-supply and sewage systems, and buildings. Major specialties within the field include structural, water resources, environmental, construction, transportation, and geotechnical engineering.

Many civil engineers hold supervisory or administrative positions, ranging from supervisor of a construction site to city engineer. Others may work in design, construction, research, and teaching.

Computer Hardware Engineers

Computer hardware engineers research, design, develop, test, and oversee the manufacture and installation of computer hardware. Hardware refers to everything from computer chips, circuit boards, and computer systems to related equipment such as keyboards, modems, and printers.

Although the work is very similar to that of electronics engineers, computer hardware engineers work exclusively with computers and computer-related equipment. The rapid advances in computer technology are largely a result of the research, development, and design efforts of these professionals.

Electrical and Electronics Engineers

Electrical and electronics engineers design, develop, test, and supervise the manufacture of electrical and electronic equipment. Electrical equipment includes power-generating and transmission equipment used by electric utilities; electric motors; machinery controls; and lighting and wiring in buildings, automobiles, and aircraft. Electronic equipment includes radar, computer hardware, and communications and video equipment.

There are several major specialties of electrical and electronics engineering, including power generation, transmission, and distribution; communications; computer electronics; and electrical equipment manufacturing. Subdivisions of these areas include industrial robot control systems or aviation electronics.

Electrical and electronics engineers design new products, write performance requirements, and develop maintenance schedules. They also test equipment, solve operating problems, and estimate the time and cost of engineering projects.

Industrial Engineers

Industrial engineers determine the most effective ways for an organization to use the basic factors of production—people, machines, materials, information, and energy—to make or process a product. They are the bridge between management and operations. They are more concerned with increasing productivity through the management of people, methods of business organization, and technology than are engineers in other specialties, who generally work more with products or processes.

To solve organizational, production, and related problems most efficiently, industrial engineers carefully study the product and its requirements, design manufacturing and information systems, and use mathematical analysis methods, such as operations research, to meet those requirements. They develop management control systems to aid in financial planning and cost analysis, design production planning and control systems to coordinate activities and control product quality, and design or improve systems for the physical distribution of goods and services.

Industrial engineers also conduct surveys to find plant locations that have the best combination of available raw materials, accessible transportation, and costs. They also develop wage and salary administration systems and job evaluation programs. Many industrial engineers move into management positions because the work is closely related.

Mechanical Engineers

Mechanical engineers design tools, engines, machines, and other mechanical equipment. They also design and develop power-producing machines such as internal combustion engines, steam and gas turbines, and jet and rocket engines. They design and develop power-using machines such as refrigeration and air-conditioning equipment, robots, machine tools, materials-handling systems, and industrial production equipment.

The work of mechanical engineers varies by industry and function. Specialties include applied mechanics, design engineering, heat transfer, power-plant engineering, pressure vessels and piping, and underwater technology. Mechanical engineers design tools needed by other engineers for their work.

Mechanical engineering is the broadest engineering discipline, extending across a variety of interdependent specialties. These engineers often work in production operations, maintenance, or technical sales; many are administrators or managers.

Metallurgical, Ceramic, and Materials Engineers

Metallurgical, ceramic, and materials engineers develop new types of metal alloys, ceramics, composites, and other materials that meet special requirements. Examples of products are graphite golf club shafts that are light but stiff, ceramic tiles on the space shuttle that protect it from burning up during reentry, and the alloy turbine blades in a jet engine.

Most metallurgical engineers work in one of the three main branches of metallurgy—extractive or chemical, physical, and mechanical or process. Extractive metallurgists are concerned with removing metals from ores and refining and alloying them to obtain useful metal. Physical metallurgists study the nature, structure, and physical properties of metals and their alloys, as well as the methods of processing them into final products. Mechanical metallurgists develop and improve metalworking processes, such as casting, forging, rolling, and drawing.

Ceramic engineers develop new ceramic materials and methods for using them to create useful products. Ceramics include all nonmetallic, inorganic materials that require high temperatures in their processing. Engineers work on products as diverse as glassware, semiconductors, automobile and aircraft engine components, fiber-optic phone lines, tile, and electric power line insulators.

Materials engineers evaluate technical requirements and material specifications to develop materials that can be used, for example, to reduce the weight, but not the strength, of an object. They also test and evaluate materials and develop new materials, such as the composite materials now being used in stealth aircraft. As another example, a materials engineer might use x-ray photoelectron spectroscopy to examine the structure of a new ceramic.

Mining Engineers

Mining engineers find, extract, and prepare metals and minerals for use by manufacturing industries. They design open pit and underground mines, supervise the construction of mine shafts and tunnels in underground operations, and devise methods for transporting minerals to processing plants. They are also responsible for the safe, economical, and environmentally sound operation of mines.

Some mining engineers work with geologists and metallurgical engineers to locate and appraise new ore deposits. Others develop new mining equipment or direct mineral processing operations to separate minerals from the dirt, rock, and other materials with which they are mixed.

Mining engineers frequently specialize in the mining of one mineral or metal, such as coal or gold. A mining engineer might also examine the plans of the current mine and those of the next phase of development to determine the best location for a conveyor system.

With increased emphasis on protecting the environment, many mining engineers work on solving problems related to land reclamation and water and air pollution.

Nuclear Engineers

Nuclear engineers conduct research on nuclear energy and radiation. They design, develop, monitor, and operate nuclear power plants used to generate electricity and power navy ships. They may work on the nuclear fuel cycle; fusion energy; the production, handling, and use of nuclear fuel; and the safe disposal of waste produced by nuclear energy.

Some nuclear engineers specialize in the development of nuclear weapons. Others develop industrial and medical uses for radioactive materials, such as equipment to diagnose and treat medical problems.

Petroleum Engineers

Petroleum engineers explore for workable reservoirs containing oil or natural gas. When one is discovered, petroleum engineers work to achieve the maximum profitable recovery from the reservoir by determining and developing the most efficient production methods.

Because only a small proportion of the oil and gas in a reservoir will flow out under natural forces, engineers develop and use various enhanced recovery methods. These include injecting water, chemicals, or steam into an oil reservoir to force more of the oil out and horizontal drilling or fracturing to connect more of a gas reservoir to a well. Since even the best methods in use today recover only a portion of the oil and gas in a reservoir, petroleum engineers work to find ways to increase this proportion.

Additional Engineering Specialties

Since engineering is a very broad field, there are branches not covered in detail here, but you can find established college curricula in these other interesting fields. Other specialties include architectural engineering (the design of a building's internal support structure), biomedical engineering (the application of engineering to medical and physiological problems), environmental engineering (a growing discipline involved with identifying, solving, and alleviating environmental problems), and marine engineering (the design and installation of ship machinery and propulsion systems).

Engineers in each branch have knowledge and training that can be applied to many fields. Electrical and electronics engineers, for example, work in the medical, computer, missile guidance, and power distribution fields. Because there are numerous problems to solve in a large engineering project, engineers in one field often work closely with specialists in other scientific, engineering, and business occupations.

Education and Training

You need at least a bachelor's degree in engineering for almost all entry-level jobs. A degree in a physical science or mathematics may qualify you for some engineering jobs, particularly in high-demand specialties.

Although most engineering degrees are granted in electrical, electronics, mechanical, or civil engineering, training in one branch may make it possible for you to work in related branches. For example, many aerospace engineers have training in mechanical engineering. This flexibility allows employers to meet staffing needs in new technologies and specialties in which engineers may be in short supply. It also allows engineers to shift to fields with better employment prospects or to those that more closely match their interests.

A typical undergraduate program involves a concentration of study in an engineering specialty, along with courses in both mathematics and the physical and life sciences. General courses not directly related to engineering, such as those in the social sciences or humanities, are usually required. Many programs also include courses in general engineering. A design course, sometimes accompanied by a computer or laboratory class or both, is part of most curricula.

In addition to the standard engineering degree, many colleges offer two- or four-year degree programs in engineering technology. These programs, which usually include various hands-on laboratory classes that focus on current issues in the application of engineering principles, are designed to prepare you for practical design and production work, rather than for jobs that require more theoretical and scientific knowledge. Completion of a four-year technology program may qualify you for jobs similar to those obtained by graduates with a bachelor's degree in engineering. An engineering technology graduate, however, is not qualified to register as a professional engineer under the same terms as graduates with degrees in engineering. Some employers regard technology program graduates as having skills between those of a technician and an engineer.

Graduate training is essential if you aspire to an engineering faculty position or many research and development programs, but is not required for the majority of entry-level engineering jobs. Many engineers obtain graduate degrees in engineering or business administration to learn new technology and broaden their education, and many high-level executives in government and industry began their careers as engineers.

You can find undergraduate programs that are accredited by the Accreditation Board for Engineering and Technology, Inc. (ABET) at about 360 colleges and universities. Approximately 230 colleges offer accredited programs in engineering technology. ABET accreditation is based on an examination of an engineering program's student achievement, program improvement, faculty, curriculum, facilities, and institutional commitment to certain principles of quality and ethics.

Although most institutions offer programs in the major branches of engineering, only a few offer programs in the smaller specialties. Also, programs of the same title may vary in content. For example, some programs emphasize industrial practices, preparing students for a job in industry, whereas others are more theoretical and are designed to prepare students for graduate work. Therefore, you should investigate curricula and check accreditations carefully before selecting a college.

In Canada, 36 educational institutions offer accredited undergraduate engineering programs leading to a bachelor's degree. There are currently 236 accredited engineering programs in a wide range of engineering disciplines. In addition to the well-known disciplines such as civil, electrical, mechanical, and chemical engineering, aspiring engineers can enter accredited programs in bioresource, computer, environmental, materials, and mining engineering, among others. Canadian programs are accredited by the Canadian Engineering Accreditation Board, which is part of the Canadian Council of Professional Engineers.

To gain admission to an undergraduate engineering school, you need a solid background in mathematics (algebra, geometry, trigonometry, and calculus) and science (biology, chemistry, and physics), with courses in English, social studies, and humanities. Bachelor's degree programs in engineering typically are designed to last four years, but many students find that it takes between four and five years to complete their studies. In a typical four-year college curriculum, you spend the first two years studying mathematics, basic sciences, introductory engineering, humanities, and social sciences. In the last two years, most courses are in engineering, usually with a concentration in one specialty. If your program offers a general engineering curriculum, you can specialize on the job or in graduate school.

There are other educational options to consider. Some engineering schools and two-year colleges have agreements under which you gain your initial engineering education at the two-year college, and the engineering school automatically admits you for your last two years. In addition, a few engineering schools have arrangements that allow you to spend three years in a liberal arts college studying pre-engineering subjects and two years in an engineering school studying core subjects and receive a bachelor's degree from each school. Some colleges and universities offer five-year master's degree programs. Some five-year or even six-year cooperative plans combine classroom study and practical work, which lets you gain valuable experience and finance part of your education.

All fifty states and the District of Columbia require licensure for engineers who offer their services directly to the public. Engineers who are licensed are called professional engineers (PE). To gain licensure, you need a degree from an ABET-accredited engineering program, four years of relevant work experience, and successful completion of a state examination. You can start the licensing process soon after graduation by taking the examination in two stages. The initial Fundamentals of Engineering (FE) exam can be taken upon graduation. Once you pass this examination, you will commonly be called an engineer in training (EIT) or engineer intern (EI). After acquiring suitable work experience, you can take the second examination, the Principles and Practice of Engineering exam.

Several states have imposed mandatory continuing education requirements for relicensure. Most states recognize licensure from other states, provided that the manner in which the initial license was obtained meets or exceeds their own requirements. Many civil, electrical, mechanical, and chemical engineers are licensed PEs. Independent of licensure, various certification programs are offered by professional organizations to demonstrate competency in specific fields of engineering.

Engineering is also a regulated profession in Canada, where all practicing engineers must be licensed. Licensing is carried out by twelve provincial and territorial associations, which set standards and regulate the profession. Although an engineering license is valid only within that jurisdiction, there is a mobility agreement among the provinces and territories regarding transfer of licenses.

Once registered as a member of a provincial or territorial association, engineers are given the designation of Professional Engineer and are eligible to use P.Eng. (or ing. in Québec) after their names. In Canada, it is illegal to practice engineering or to use the P.Eng./ing. designation without being licensed as a member in a professional association.

To have a successful career in engineering, you should be creative, inquisitive, analytical, detail oriented, able to work as part of a team, and able to communicate well, both orally and in writing. Communication abilities are important because interaction with specialists in a wide range of fields outside engineering is common.

As a new engineering graduate, you'll most likely work under the supervision of experienced engineers and, in large companies, may also receive formal classroom or seminar-type training. As you gain knowledge and experience, you'll be assigned more difficult projects with greater independence to develop designs, solve problems, and make decisions. As your career progresses, you may advance to become a technical specialist, to supervise a staff or team of engineers and technicians, or, eventually, to become an engineering manager or enter other managerial or sales jobs.

Job Outlook

Engineers have traditionally been concentrated in slow-growing manufacturing industries, in which they will continue to be needed to design, build, test, and improve manufactured products. However, increasing employment of engineers in faster-growing service industries should generate a majority of the employment growth. Overall job opportunities are expected to be favorable because the number of engineering graduates should be in rough balance with the number of job openings over the next decade, but the job outlook varies by specialty.

Competitive pressures and advancing technology will force companies to improve and update product designs and to optimize their manufacturing processes, and employers will rely on engineers to further increase productivity as investment in plants and equipment increases to expand output of goods and services. New technologies continue to improve the design process, enabling engineers to produce and analyze various product designs much more rapidly than in the past.

Unlike in other fields, however, technological advances are not expected to limit employment opportunities substantially, because they will allow the development of new products and processes.

There are many well-trained, often English-speaking engineers available around the world willing to work at much lower salaries than are U.S. engineers. The rise of the Internet has made it relatively easy for much of the engineering work previously done by engineers in this country to be done by engineers in other countries, a factor that will tend to hold down employment growth. Even so, the need for on-site engineers to interact with other employees and with clients will remain.

Many engineers work on long-term research and development projects or in other activities that continue even during economic slowdowns. In industries such as electronics and aerospace, however, large cutbacks in defense expenditures and in government funding for research and development have resulted in significant layoffs of engineers in the past. The trend toward contracting for engineering work with engineering services firms, both domestic and foreign, has had the same result.

It is important for engineers to continue their education throughout their careers because much of their value to their employer depends on their knowledge of the latest technology. Engineers in high-technology areas, such as advanced electronics or information technology, may find that technical knowledge can become outdated rapidly. By keeping current in the field, engineers are able to deliver the best solutions and greatest value to their employers. Those who have not kept current may find themselves passed over for promotions or vulnerable to layoffs.

Salaries

Earnings for engineers vary significantly by specialty, industry, and education. Even so, engineers earn some of the highest average starting salaries among those with bachelor's degrees. Table 1 shows average starting salaries for engineers, according to a 2005 survey by the National Association of Colleges and Employers.

TABLE 1. Starting Salaries for Engineers

CURRICULUM	BACHELOR'S	MASTER'S	DOCTORATE
Aerospace/aeronautical	$50,993	$62,930	$72,529
Chemical	$53,813	$57,260	$79,591
Civil	$43,679	$48,050	$59,625
Computer	$52,464	$60,354	$69,625
Electrical and electronics	$51,888	$64,416	$80,206
Industrial	$49,567	$56,561	$85,000
Mechanical	$50,236	$59,880	$68,229
Metallurgic, ceramic, and materials	$50,982		
Mining	$48,643		
Nuclear	$51,182	$58,814	
Petroleum	$61,516		

Source: National Association of Colleges and Employers

In the federal government, mean annual salaries for engineers ranged from $100,059 in ceramic engineering to $70,086 in agricultural engineering in 2005.

· ·
Parade of Professionals

Read the accounts of the following professionals to see whether a career in engineering might be right for you.

Krista Jacobsen, Ph.D., Electrical Engineer

Dr. Krista Jacobsen is senior systems engineer at Amati Communications Corporation in San Jose, California. She received her B.S. degree in electrical engineering from the University of Denver and both her M.S. and Ph.D. in electrical engineering from Stanford University.

Dr. Jacobsen was attracted to electrical engineering because she found those courses to be the most challenging. "I worked harder than I ever had in school, and the extra effort paid off," she says. "Not only did I graduate with all As in major courses, but I was awarded scholarships to an outstanding graduate school and also awarded graduate fellowships."

Dr. Jacobsen worked at Amati Communications as a consultant while pursuing her doctorate, and the company offered her a position when she earned her degree. She describes her job as somewhat unusual for an electrical engineer, because her employer considers her quite versatile and assigns her tasks not traditionally associated with her specialty. Her particular responsibilities include designing and managing the company's website; writing and running computer simulations to project the performance of the company's systems; and investigating alternative solutions and design of new products. She also attends standards meetings for which she writes and presents technical contributions, and she provides technical support as necessary to the sales and marketing departments, which frequently requires travel to other companies or to conferences.

When asked what advice she would give to prospective engineers, Dr. Jacobsen suggests, "Work hard so you can reap the rewards. Many people drop out of engineering programs because some of the courses seem so difficult. The key is to survive the nasty courses and excel in the courses that you enjoy. The road gets easier and more interesting as you progress, and eventually you'll find out that a career in engineering is fun, rewarding, and challenging."

Carol Prochnow, Computer Engineer

Carol Prochnow is senior section manager at Schlumberger Well Services. She received her bachelor of science degree in electrical and computer engineering from the University of Michigan in Ann Arbor and her master of science degree in computer science from Cornell University in Ithaca, New York.

When Carol was in high school, the computing profession was still in its infancy. Her brother was taking a class on the FORTRAN programming language, and she looked at the textbook and became fascinated by the idea of programming. Computer science seemed very attractive and looked like a career that would be viable for many years.

In her present position, Carol is an engineering manager for about twenty people. Her staff is responsible for the data acquisition and analysis software for a service industry called "oil well logging," the company's core business. "When an oil company drills a well, it isn't like in movies when a huge gusher begins to spew oil into the sky," she explains. "In fact, they sometimes do not know if there are hydrocarbons or where they are." Schlumberger is hired to lower advanced sensors into the oil well bore, connected via a conducting cable to a computer system on the surface. Carol's section is responsible for the "middleware" software that sits on top of this computer's operating system. This software provides data acquisition, data management, task control, and graphics facilities to support different sensors. It is loaded into the computer system either in a truck or an offshore unit.

A typical day is spent dealing with e-mail, attending meetings, reviewing documents, and talking on the phone. When Carol misses being an engineer, she'll go in and fix a software bug. Since she loves to build things, she's glad that this is an integral part of the job. The team sees projects all the way from requirements analysis through delivery to the company's field organization.

Carol has some suggestions for others interested in engineering. "I would advise interested candidates to get good grades," she says. "Grades are what you need to get your foot in the door of a good job. Schlumberger does not even look at resumes that have less than a B+ average. Continuing your education is always a plus, and internships are very valuable. In my own case, I feel that my master's degree helped me to get this job and also provided me with some skills I didn't have when I finished my undergraduate program.

"It's a good idea to work at a variety of companies during summer breaks. You'll learn a lot and also find out if you like working with the same individuals day after day. If not, engineering is probably not for you."

Mary Shafer, Aerospace Engineer

Mary Shafer is a senior aerospace engineer for NASA at the Dryden Flight Research Center, which is considered NASA's premier installation for aeronautical flight research. Located at Edwards Air Force Base in California's Mojave Desert, the center has grown from an initial group of five engineers in 1946 to a facility with more than 460 NASA government employees and about the same number of civilian contractor personnel. In addition to carrying out aeronautical research, Dryden also supports the space shuttle program as a primary and backup landing site and as a facility to test and validate design concepts and systems used in both development and operation.

As a high school senior, Mary attended a National Science Foundation course at UCLA. The subject was meteorology, and it gave her a chance to see that science and research provided a way to explain the world, which she felt was interesting and important. Mary got a summer job working for the air force, where she discovered that she liked being near airplanes. She began her college career at UCLA as a chemistry major but later switched to engineering and spent subsequent summers working for NASA.

This experience helped her to decide that she wanted to focus her career on airplanes and flight research. Mary felt very fortunate to work with many good people who were willing to explain things and provide her with examples in everyday life that related to aerodynamics and fluid mechanics.

In her summer jobs at NASA, Mary began by reducing data, working with a ruler in engineering units, plotting the information on graph paper with orange carbon behind it. She wrote a couple of smaller programs and the next year progressed to writing computer matrix manipulations designed to measure trial time stability analysis during flight. She found this particularly interesting because it was at that point that she began to understand the rules that govern how airplanes fly.

After earning her bachelor's degree, Mary worked another summer writing quality programs for some of the engineers. She got her master's degree and the following summer was writing with engineers and even married one.

Mary began working as a computer programmer writing follow-up programs for the X-24B, then worked for Lockheed on the FA certification of the L-1011. She moved on to McDonnell Douglas and McDonnell Aircraft, working on the F-4 airplane and the initial acceptance testing of the F-15. Next she accepted a position in the air force as a systems designer working on writing programs, and she finally returned to NASA as a controls engineer.

NASA employs aeronautical engineers, mechanical engineers, electrical engineers, meteorologists, and physicists. Mary stresses that it's vital for anyone hoping to work for the agency to know math and how to program and use the computer. The ability to write clearly and with accurate grammar is also important. She says, "There's no point in doing research if you can't write it down clearly and concisely enough that people can understand what you did, how you did it, why you did it, and what happened when you did it. Flexibility is another important quality for researchers because you don't know how your attempts are going to come out, and you have to be able to build upon your successes or shift gears when the outcome isn't as you planned. People who are unable to deal with uncertainty may find that research is not a good field for them. And in this line of work, a robust ego is a nice thing to have."

Mary works on various projects. For example, in addition to a number of small flying-qualities research projects, she is working on one particular experiment called the aerospy. It is her responsibility to look at an airplane's various flying qualities to make sure that any modifications that are made are safe.

Most of Mary's day is spent either talking with pilots, studying data on various computers, visiting the simulation area to see how the plane is flying, and watching the input of new ideas. The results of the research are put into a simulator, so that the pilots can test them and determine if the real planes will fly as expected. For example, the engineers focus on questions such as: "Are we going to have enough runway to take off?" "Are we going to have enough thrust?" "Will it go forward instead of falling out of the sky?"

Mary works fairly regular hours, although there are occasionally surges in the workload that require her to work on weekends. One example is when she needs to write a paper documenting a research project.

Mary describes research as essentially a mutual endeavor. She says, "When you begin a project, you never really know what will be gained from your efforts, what will be gleaned, or how the new information might be used. It is only in the later stages of your work that you may be able to ascertain exactly how the information gained from your research will affect others on a grander scale. This is what provides fulfillment for all scientists and engineers—uncovering or discovering information that can benefit the world in which we live."

Lieutenant Colonel Joseph W. McVeigh, Aeronautical Engineer

Lieutenant Colonel Joseph W. McVeigh is chief of the operations division of the U.S. Army's Air Worthiness Qualification Test Directorate at Edwards Air Force Base in California. He'd always wanted to fly and decided the best way to achieve this was to join one of the armed services.

Lieutenant Colonel McVeigh attended the University of Montana in Missoula, where he joined Army ROTC in his sophomore year and earned a B.S. in forestry. He later received an M.A. in computer resource management from Webster University in St. Louis, Missouri. Once he graduated and was commissioned as a second lieutenant, he was sent to Fort Knox, Kentucky, for the Army Officer's Basic Course. He applied for flight school and was accepted. On his first flying assignment, he was selected to support an aviation test for a new type of radio. The test lasted three months and made him realize that this was what he wanted to do in the army. He was assigned to the Aviation Board in Fort Rucker, Alabama.

In previous jobs at Fort Rucker, Lieutenant Colonel McVeigh worked as a test project officer, where he conducted operational tests on several aircraft-related components, and as a UH-60 plans officer, where he initiated test plans for operational testing for future programs. He moved to the aviation systems command in St. Louis, where he worked as an aeronautical engineer on the design of various cockpits to provide human factors input on design, layout, and safety-of-flight crucial items. His second job in St. Louis focused on performing administrative work for two general officers and then shifted to coordinating joint programs with the navy and air force intended to allow all three military branches to use the same equipment in the future. He also worked in Canada, England, and Saudi Arabia to initiate joint laboratory work between these countries and the army.

The Army's Acquisition Corps is made up of a small group of officers (approximately two thousand from the rank of captain to colonel) who come from all branches of the army (infantry, aviation, field artillery, and so forth). The purpose of the Acquisition Corps is to have an elite group of officers that procures all of the equipment, weapons, and vehicles that the army requires for its operations. This includes research and development, test and evaluation, program management, and staff/support functions.

Lieutenant Colonel McVeigh explains that the army differentiates between research and development (R&D) and test evaluation (T&E). The research and development personnel work in the army laboratories and at universities doing basic research and concept exploration. He works in the test evaluation area, which conducts developmental testing of hardware (testing to specifications) and operational testing (testing with troops to determine operational stability).

Currently stationed at Edwards Air Force Base with U.S. Army Airworthiness Qualification Test Directorate, Lieutenant Colonel McVeigh conducts airworthiness flight testing of army helicopters and airplanes. When he first arrived, he performed as a flight test engineer, which included work on the OH-58D helicopter and the MH-47E helicopter.

As a flight test engineer he was in charge of the flights, telling the experimental test pilots what profile to fly, how to fly it, and for how long. Designing the test plan was one of his major responsibilities; it was the road map that everyone would follow to conduct the test. He also coordinated the flight crews and crash rescue crews, test budgets, and personnel overtime.

On a typical day as a flight test engineer, he arrived at work at 7 A.M. to pick up where he'd left off on reducing data from the previous day's (or week's) flights. If a test flight was scheduled for that day for his aircraft, he briefed the crews, maintenance personnel, safety and crash rescue, and flight operations personnel on the schedule for the day. He would then coordinate the aircraft's preparation for the flight, prepare the flight data card, operate the test equipment and data recording equipment on board, and queue the pilots on what to do next during the flight. If another engineer had a flight, he would fly a chase aircraft alongside for safety. The chase pilot coordinates the airspace and makes all the radio calls to ground and air traffic control and range control.

After a year as flight test engineer, he was selected for his current position as chief of the operations division. He is in charge of the organization's budget, flight operations, photography and graphic arts support, technical publications support, and business office. In addition, he flies in support of flight tests at Edwards and at other remote sites under the army's jurisdiction.

"This type of career is designed for a particular type of person," Lieutenant Colonel McVeigh says, "one who is dedicated to his or her work and who sees things in a larger perspective, one who wants to provide the world with something better than what we already have."

Ernestine Meyers, Environmental Engineer

Ernestine Meyers serves as senior environmental engineer for the Division of Sanitation Facilities Construction in the Office of Environmental Health and Engineering of the Indian Health Service in Albuquerque, New Mexico.

Ernestine's father worked for the Indian Health Service as an environmental health technician. As a child, she spent summers in the field with him, traveling to different reservations where she met and talked with engineers and learned about their responsibilities. "With my father as a role model and a love for science and the outdoors, I found my career direction," she says.

Ernestine was born on a New Mexico pueblo reservation, so she had the option of attending the Bureau of Indian Affairs school or a public school nearby. She chose the public school, where she took all the college preparatory classes she'd need to ensure acceptance at a college or university. Even in high school, she enjoyed science and knew it would be her major concentration.

During the summer of her junior year in high school, Ernestine attended the Minority Introduction to Engineering course at New Mexico State University. The course introduced her to all the different types of engineering, but civil engineering quickly became her choice because she loved the outdoors and knew she wouldn't be happy spending all her time at a desk or computer.

After high school, Ernestine enrolled at New Mexico State University with a four-year Professional Guild Scholarship from the U.S. Department of Health and Human Services. The scholarship paid for all of her undergraduate education, and in return she was obligated to work for the agency for four years after graduation. With her bachelor of science in environmental engineering, Ernestine was assigned to a Navajo reservation in the city of Tuba, Arizona.

As a field engineer, she was responsible for planning and organizing the construction of sanitation facilities and bringing in water lines for individual families. She found this work very rewarding, and when she left, the Navajo tribe presented her with an achievement medal for the work she did during those four years.

Another of Ernestine's focuses is her membership in the Commission Corps of the Public Health Service, one of the branches of the military. After finishing her undergraduate degree, she had a choice of entering employment through the civil service or applying for the Commission Corps. She chose the Commission Corps because she felt that it would provide better opportunities for advancement and today holds the rank of lieutenant commander.

Ernestine transferred to the Pacific Northwest, where she worked with three different tribes, assuming the same duties she'd previously held in Arizona. She was the only field engineer in the office, and although this was initially intimidating, she learned to work independently. She was even selected as the engineer of the year for the Portland area.

After three years, the Indian Health Service chose Ernestine to complete long-term training to earn her master's degree in environmental engineering. The offer allowed her to attend school for one year and still receive her regular salary, with all educational expenses absorbed by the agency. She returned to New Mexico State University, where she dedicated herself to the challenge of completing a two-year program in one year.

A typical day consists of working on the plans and designs for a pueblo springhouse, spending time with the surveyors who are doing the groundwork for some of her projects, working on specifications or proposals for future projects, dealing with contractors, or helping out the other engineers when they have any technical questions.

Ernestine's next goal is to obtain her professional registration. To accomplish this, she'll need to take an eight-hour exam that covers all areas of engineering. Once she earns the registration, she will be eligible for promotion.

"The advice I would give others is to stress that you need to persevere." Ernestine says. "I was determined to get my degree no matter what. And I had some hard times in college where I thought, 'Oh, I'm not going to pass this class.' I used to worry about this. But I always managed to do all right. I relied on friends or sought out help from teachers. It's not easy, but nothing that's worth accomplishing ever is. Every time you reach a goal you've set for yourself, it's time to set another.

"When I went back for my master's degree (where you must maintain a B average or better), I realized I could have worked a lot harder as an undergraduate. You should always do the best you can. Just meeting minimum standards is not good enough."

Cristina Calderon, Civil Engineer

Cristina Calderon is a transportation engineer for the city and county of San Francisco, Department of Parking and Traffic. She received her bachelor of science degree in civil engineering from Santa Clara University in California and is registered in California as an Engineer in Training (EIT).

Cristina first learned about civil engineering from her fifth grade teacher, who knew that she liked math and science and wanted a career that would allow her to use both subjects. While in high school, she attended Santa Clara University's Summer Engineering Seminar and learned more about civil engineering as a major in college and as a career. In college, she concentrated on both structural and transportation engineering.

After college, Cristina served as project engineer for a construction company, an area she chose because she wanted to see a project built from the ground to completion. Her first project was building two hotels on the same site—a seven-story, reinforced concrete, post-tensioned slab hotel and a four-story wood-frame hotel.

Cristina was hired for her current job as a direct result of serving an internship there during college. The work is highly technical and very involved. She is working on developing an Integrated Transportation Management System (ITMS) using the latest Intelligent Transportation System (ITS) technology. The project involves a great deal of coordination, and on a typical day Cristina has meetings with consultants, the board of supervisors, vendors, or her own project team. She describes the work atmosphere as often intense but comfortable, thanks to the attitudes of the team members. The average workweek is forty hours, but she could easily work longer hours.

What Cristina likes most about her job is working with state-of-the-art technology and with a great project team. What she likes least is that she is often frustrated at the rate at which things occur, although she understands that this is often the result of working with new technology.

Cristina works as a civil engineer because she likes to solve problems by applying her skills in math and science as well as those derived from practical experience. She also enjoys the daily challenges that the work provides. Once she's gained more experience, she plans to earn her master's degree and continue to work in design.

"My advice to other scientific types who are still in school is to gain as much experience as possible in your desired career," Cristina says. "I particularly recommend internships and co-ops because they provide a comfortable way to decide if this is really what you wish to make your life's work. Besides, they can even lead to jobs after graduation. Mine did."

For More Information

High school students who are interested in obtaining general information on a variety of engineering disciplines should contact the Junior Engineering Technical Society (JETS):

JETS
1420 King Street, Suite 405
Alexandria, VA 22314
www.jets.org

High school students interested in obtaining information on ABET-accredited engineering programs should contact:

ABET (Accreditation Board for Engineering and Technology)
111 Market Place, Suite 1050
Baltimore, MD 21202
www.abet.org

Canadian Federation of Engineering Students
www.cfes.ca

For more detailed information about the individual branches of
engineering, contact the following professional associations.

Aerospace Industries Association of Canada
60 Queen Street, Suite 1200
Ottawa, ON K1P 5Y7
Canada
www.aiac.ca

American Institute of Aeronautics and Astronautics
1801 Alexander Bell Drive, Suite 500
Reston, VA 20191
www.aiaa.org

American Institute of Chemical Engineers
3 Park Avenue
New York, NY 10016
www.aiche.org

American Chemical Society
Department of Career Services
1155 Sixteenth Street NW
Washington, DC 20036
www.chemistry.org

American Nuclear Society
555 North Kensington Avenue
La Grange Park, IL 60526
www.ans.org

American Society of Civil Engineers
1801 Alexander Bell Drive
Reston, VA 20191
www.asce.org

American Society of Heating, Refrigerating, and
  Air-Conditioning Engineers
1791 Tullie Circle NE
Atlanta, GA 30329
www.ashrae.org

The American Society of Mechanical Engineers
3 Park Avenue
New York, NY 10016
www.asme.org

ASM International (The Materials Information Society)
9639 Kinsman Road
Materials Park, OH 44073
www.asminternational.org

Canadian Geotechnical Society
PO Box 937
Alliston, ON L9R 1W1
Canada
www.cgs.ca

Canadian Nuclear Society
480 University Avenue, Suite 200
Toronto, ON M5G 1V2
Canada
www.cns-snc.ca

Canadian Society for Chemical Engineering
13 Rue Slater Street, Suite 550
Ottawa, ON K1P 6E2
Canada
www.chemeng.ca

Canadian Society for Civil Engineering
4920 de Maisonneuve Boulevard West, Suite 201
Montréal, QC H3Z 1N1
Canada
www.csce.ca

Institute of Electrical and Electronics Engineers
445 Hoes Lane
Piscataway, NJ 08854
www.ieee.org

Institute of Industrial Engineers
3577 Parkway Lane, Suite 200
Norcross, GA 30092
www.iienet.org

The Minerals, Metals & Materials Society
184 Thornhill Road
Warrendale, PA 15086
www.tms.org

Society for Mining, Metallurgy, and Exploration
8307 Shaffer Parkway
Littleton, CO 80127
www.smenet.org

Society of Petroleum Engineers
PO Box 833836
Richardson, TX 75083
www.spe.org

Information on acquiring a job as an engineer with the federal government may be obtained from the Office of Personnel Management. Visit the website at www.usajobs.com. In Canada, visit www.jobs-emplois.gc.ca for federal job postings.

CHAPTER SIX

Careers in Computer Science and Mathematics

*The new electronic interdependence re-creates the world
in the image of a global village.*
—Marshall McLuhan

*Mathematics possesses not only truth, but supreme beauty
—a beauty cold and austere, like that of a sculpture.*
—Bertrand Russell

Career possibilities in the world of computers are incredibly plentiful and varied, and chronicles of success flourish. Perhaps the most dramatic story of all is one that most of us know bits and pieces of already: Bill Gates, chairperson, cofounder, and CEO of Microsoft Corporation in Redmond, Washington. By the time he was twelve, Gates was already intrigued by computers. During his high school years, he worked in the mainframe and minicomputer programming field, and in college he worked with Paul Allen to develop the BASIC programming language for the first commercially available microcomputer, the MITS Altair. He and Allen went on to form Microsoft Corporation in 1975. The company has been so successful that, according to a *New York Times* article, more than two thousand of the company's employees are estimated to be millionaires.

Microsoft had revenues of $39.79 billion for the fiscal year ending June 2005 and employs more than sixty-one thousand people in 102 countries and regions. Bill Gates is reputed to be the wealthiest man in America. In June 2006, the company announced that effective July 2008 Gates will transition out of a day-to-day role in the company to spend more time on his global health and education work at the Bill & Melinda Gates Foundation. He will continue to serve as Microsoft's chairperson and an advisor on key development projects.

If your scientific mind leans toward the world of computers and computer science, read on.

Computer Science Professionals

The rapid spread of computers and information technology in the last twenty-five years has generated a need for highly trained workers proficient in a variety of job functions. These workers—computer scientists, database administrators, and network systems and data communication analysts—include a wide range of computer specialists. Because this is such a rapidly growing field, job tasks and occupational titles used to describe these workers evolve rapidly, reflecting new areas of specialization or changes in technology, as well as the preferences and practices of employers.

Computer Scientists

Computer scientists work as theorists, researchers, or inventors. Their jobs are distinguished by the higher level of theoretical expertise and innovation they apply to complex problems and the creation or application of new technology. Those employed by academic institutions work in areas ranging from complexity theory to hardware to programming-language design. Some work on multidisciplinary projects, such as developing and advancing uses of virtual reality, extending human-computer interaction, or designing robots. Their counterparts in private industry work in areas such as applying theory; developing specialized languages or information technologies; or designing programming tools, knowledge-based systems, or even computer games.

Database Administrators

With the Internet and electronic business generating large volumes of data, there is a growing need to be able to store, manage, and extract data effectively. Database administrators work with database management systems software and determine ways to organize and store data. They identify user requirements, set up computer databases, and test and coordinate modifications to the computer database systems. An organization's database administrator ensures the performance of the system, understands the platform on which the database runs, and adds new users to the system. Because they also may design and implement system security, database administrators often plan and coordinate security measures. With the volume of sensitive data generated every second growing rapidly, data integrity, backup systems, and database security have become increasingly important aspects of the job.

Network Systems and Data Communications Analysts

Because networks are configured in many ways, network systems and data communications analysts are needed to design, test, and evaluate systems such as local area networks (LANs), wide area networks (WANs), the Internet, and intranets. Systems can range from a connection between two offices in the same building to globally distributed networks, voice mail, and e-mail systems of a multinational organization. Network systems and data communications analysts perform network modeling, analysis, and planning; they also may research related products and make necessary hardware and software recommendations.

Telecommunications Specialists

Telecommunications specialists focus on the interaction between computer and communications equipment. They design voice and data communication systems, supervise the installation of the systems, and provide maintenance and other services to clients after the systems are installed.

Internet and Web Specialists

The growth of the Internet and the expansion of the World Wide Web (the graphical portion of the Internet) have generated a variety of occupations related to the design, development, and maintenance of websites and their servers. For example, webmasters are responsible for all technical aspects of a website, including performance issues such as speed of access, and for approving the content of the site. Internet developers or Web developers, also called Web designers, are responsible for day-to-day site creation and design.

Mathematicians

Mathematicians use mathematical theory, computational techniques, algorithms, and the latest computer technology to solve economic, scientific, engineering, physics, and business problems. Their work falls into two broad classes—theoretical (pure) mathematics and applied mathematics. However, these classes are not sharply defined and often overlap.

Theoretical Mathematicians

Theoretical mathematicians advance mathematical knowledge by developing new principles and by recognizing previously unknown relationships between existing principles of mathematics. Although they seek to increase basic knowledge without necessarily considering its practical use, such pure and abstract knowledge has been instrumental in producing or furthering many scientific and engineering achievements. Many theoretical mathematicians are employed as university faculty, dividing their time between teaching and conducting research.

Applied Mathematicians

Applied mathematicians use theories and techniques, such as mathematical modeling and computational methods, to formulate and solve practical problems in business, government, and engineering, and in the physical, life, and social sciences. For example, they may analyze the most efficient way to schedule airline routes between cities, the effects and safety of new drugs, the aerodynamic characteristics of an experimental automobile, or the cost-effectiveness of alternative manufacturing processes.

Those working in industrial research and development may develop or enhance mathematical methods when solving a difficult problem. Some mathematicians, called cryptanalysts, analyze and decipher encryption systems designed to transmit military, political, financial, or law enforcement–related information in code.

Applied mathematicians start with a practical problem, envision the separate elements of the process under consideration, and then reduce the elements to mathematical variables. They often use computers to analyze relationships among the variables and solve complex problems by developing models with alternative solutions.

Much of the work in applied mathematics is done by people with titles other than mathematician. For example, engineers, computer scientists, physicists, and economists are among those who use mathematics extensively. Some professionals, including statisticians, actuaries, and operations research analysts, actually are specialists in a particular branch of mathematics. Frequently, applied mathematicians are required to collaborate with other workers in their organizations to achieve common solutions to problems.

Education and Training

These interesting careers require specific education and training. Read on and explore whether your scientific mind is drawn to any of these programs of study.

Computer Scientists and Related Professionals

In order to pursue a career in computer science, you have to keep up with rapidly changing technology that requires an increasing level of skill and education. A broad background and range of skills, including not only technical knowledge but also communication and other interpersonal skills, is attractive to many employers.

While there is no universally accepted way to prepare for a job as a network systems analyst, computer scientist, or database administrator, most employers place a premium on some formal college education. You need a bachelor's degree to be qualified for many jobs, although a two-year degree may be enough for some positions. Although many employers prefer to hire those with technical degrees, you can still enter this field with a degree in a variety of majors. Employers also look for relevant work experience. For example, graduates with formal education or experience in information security are currently in demand.

If you're interested in a career as a database administrator, you should consider earning a bachelor's degree in computer science, information science, or management information systems (MIS). Most MIS programs are part of the business school or college and differ considerably from computer science programs, emphasizing business and management-oriented course work and business computing courses. A master's degree in business administration with a concentration in information systems is also valuable, as more firms are moving their business to the Internet.

An associate's degree or a two-year certificate is sufficient for some network systems and data communication analyst positions, although more advanced positions might require a computer-related bachelor's degree. Computer and information scientists generally need a doctoral degree because of the highly technical nature of the work.

The level of education and the type of training needed for specific jobs depends on employers' needs, which are often affected by changes in technology. Workers with formal education or experience in information security, for example, are in demand because of the growing need for their skills and services. Workers skilled in wireless technologies are also in demand because wireless networks and applications have spread into many firms and organizations.

You can find associate's degree programs at most community colleges and many independent technical institutes and proprietary schools. Many of these programs may be geared more toward meeting the needs of local businesses and are more occupation specific than four-year degree programs, and some jobs may be better suited to the level of training that such programs offer.

Employers usually look for people who have broad knowledge and experience related to computer systems and technologies, strong problem-solving and analytical skills, and good interpersonal skills. Courses in computer science or systems design provide good preparation for a job in computer occupations. For jobs in a business environment, employers usually want systems analysts to have business management or closely related skills, while a background in the physical sciences, applied mathematics, or engineering is preferred for work in scientifically oriented organizations. Art or graphic design skills may be desirable for webmasters or Web developers.

You can enhance your employment opportunities by participating in internship or co-op programs offered through your school. You might develop advanced computer skills in a field other than computers and transfer those skills to a computer occupation. For this reason, a background in the industry in which you gain your computer skills, such as banking, accounting, or financial services, can be important. You may also take computer science courses to supplement your study in fields such as accounting, inventory control, or other business areas.

To work as a computer scientist or database administrator, you must be able to think logically and have good communication skills. The ability to concentrate and pay close attention to detail is important, because you often must deal with a number of tasks simultaneously. Although you sometimes work independently, you frequently work in teams on large projects and must be able to communicate effectively with computer personnel, such as programmers and managers, as well as with users or other staff who may have no technical computer background.

Computer scientists employed in private industry may advance into managerial or project leadership positions. Those employed in academic institutions can become heads of research departments or published authorities in their field. Database administrators may advance into managerial positions, such as chief technology officer, on the basis of their experience managing data and enforcing security. Computer specialists with work experience and considerable expertise in a particular subject or a certain application may find lucrative opportunities as independent consultants or may choose to start their own computer consulting firms.

Technological advances come so rapidly in the computer field that continuous study is necessary to keep your skills up to date. Employers, hardware and software vendors, colleges and universities, and private training institutions offer continuing education. You can also get additional training from professional development seminars offered by professional computing societies.

Certification is a way to demonstrate a level of competence in your field. Some product vendors or software firms offer certification and require professionals who work with their products to be certified—many employers regard these certifications as the industry standard. For example, one method of acquiring enough knowledge to get a job as a database administrator is to become certified in a specific type of database management. Voluntary certification also is available through various organizations associated with computer specialists. Professional certification may give you a competitive advantage in your job search.

Mathematicians

You need a doctorate in mathematics for most jobs, except in the federal government, where entry-level job candidates usually must have a four-year degree with a major in mathematics or a four-year degree with the equivalent of a mathematics major (twenty-four semester hours of mathematics courses).

If you aspire to a job in private industry, you typically need a doctorate, although a master's degree may qualify you for some jobs. Most of the positions designated for mathematicians are as part of technical teams in research and development laboratories. Mathematicians in these settings engage either in basic research on pure mathematical principles or in applied research on developing or improving specific products or processes. The majority of those with bachelor's or master's degrees in mathematics who work in private industry actually have titles such as computer programmer, systems analyst, or systems engineer.

You can find bachelor's degree programs in mathematics at most colleges and universities. Your courses will include calculus, differential equations, and linear and abstract algebra, with additional classes in probability theory and statistics, mathematical analysis, numerical analysis, topology, discrete mathematics, and mathematical logic. Depending on your school's policies, you may be required to take courses in a field that is closely related to mathematics, such as computer science, engineering, life science, physical science, or economics. A double major in mathematics and another related discipline is particularly desirable to many employers. If you plan to major in mathematics in college, you'll find it helpful to take as many math courses as possible while in high school.

In 2004, about two hundred colleges and universities offered a master's degree as the highest degree in either pure or applied mathematics; about two hundred offered a doctorate in pure or applied mathematics. In graduate school, you will conduct research and take advanced courses, usually specializing in a subfield of mathematics.

For jobs in applied mathematics, you should pursue training in the field in which the mathematics will be used. For example, mathematics is used extensively in physics, actuarial science, statistics, engineering, and operations research. Computer science, business and industrial management, economics, finance, chemistry, geology, life sciences, and behavioral sciences are likewise dependent on applied mathematics. You also should have substantial knowledge of computer programming because most complex mathematical computations and much mathematical modeling are done on a computer.

To succeed in a career in mathematics, you need good reasoning ability and persistence in order to identify, analyze, and apply basic principles to technical problems. Communication skills also are important, as you must be able to interact and discuss proposed solutions with people who may not have extensive knowledge of mathematics.

Job Outlook

What are the job prospects in these interesting fields? Read on to see the projections for the next few years.

Computer Science Professionals

Computer scientists and related professionals should continue to enjoy favorable job prospects. However, as technology becomes more sophisticated and complex, employers demand a higher level of skill and expertise. An advanced degree in computer science or computer engineering or a master's in business administration with a concentration in information systems should make your prospects more favorable. A bachelor's degree in computer science, computer engineering, information science, or MIS should also lead to good prospects, particularly if you have supplemented your formal education with practical experience.

Because employers continue to seek computer specialists who can combine strong technical skills with good interpersonal and business skills, graduates with degrees in fields other than computer science who have had courses in computer programming, systems analysis, and other information technology areas also should continue to find jobs in these computer fields. In fact, those with the right experience and training can work in these computer occupations regardless of their college major or level of formal education.

Computer specialists are expected to be among the fastest-growing occupations through 2014, as organizations continue to adopt and integrate increasingly sophisticated technologies. Job increases will be driven by very rapid growth in computer systems design and related services, which is projected to be one of the fastest-growing industries in the U.S. economy. Job growth will not be as rapid as during the previous decade, however, as the information technology sector begins to mature and as routine work is increasingly outsourced overseas.

The demand for networking to facilitate the sharing of information, the expansion of client-server environments, and the need for computer specialists to use their knowledge and skills in a problem-solving capacity will be major factors in the rising demand for computer professionals. Moreover, falling prices of computer hardware and software should continue to induce more businesses to expand their computerized operations and integrate new technologies into them. To maintain a competitive edge and operate more efficiently, firms will keep demanding computer specialists who are knowledgeable about the latest technologies and are able to apply them to meet the needs of businesses.

Increasingly, organizations are implementing more sophisticated and complex technology. There is growing demand for network systems and data communication analysts to help firms maximize their efficiency with available technology. Expansion of electronic commerce and the continuing need to build and maintain databases that store critical information on customers, inventory, and projects are fueling demand for database administrators familiar with the latest technology. Also, the increasing importance placed on cyber security—the protection of electronic information—will result in a need for workers skilled in information security.

The development of new technologies usually leads to demand for various kinds of workers. For example, the expanding integration of Internet technologies into businesses has resulted in a growing need for specialists who can develop and support Internet and intranet applications. The growth of electronic commerce means that more establishments use the Internet to conduct their business online. The introduction of the wireless Internet, known as Wi-Fi, creates new systems to be analyzed and new data to be administered. The spread of such new technologies translates into a need for information technology professionals who can help organizations use technology to communicate with employees, clients, and consumers. Explosive growth in these areas also is expected to fuel demand for specialists who are knowledgeable about network, data, and communications security.

Mathematicians

Employment of mathematicians is expected to decline through 2014, reflecting the reduction in the number of jobs with the title mathematician. As a result, competition is expected to be keen for the limited number of jobs. You will have the best opportunity if you have a master's or doctorate with a strong background in mathematics and a related discipline, such as engineering or computer science. Many who work in these areas have job titles that reflect their occupation, such as systems analyst, rather than the title mathematician, reflecting their primary educational background.

Advancements in technology usually lead to expanding applications of mathematics, and more workers with knowledge of mathematics will be required in the future. However, jobs in industry and government often require advanced knowledge of related scientific disciplines in addition to mathematics, the most common fields being computer science and software development, physics, engineering, and operations research.

More mathematicians also are becoming involved in financial analysis. However, mathematicians must compete for jobs with people who have degrees in these other disciplines. The most successful candidates will be able to apply mathematical theory to real-world problems and will possess good communication, teamwork, and computer skills.

To work in private industry jobs, you will need at least a master's degree in mathematics or in a related field. A bachelor's degree in mathematics is usually not qualification enough for most jobs, and many seek advanced degrees in mathematics or a related discipline. However, bachelor's degree holders who meet state certification requirements may become primary or secondary school mathematics teachers.

Those with master's degrees in mathematics will face strong competition for jobs in theoretical research. Because the number of doctorates awarded in mathematics continues to exceed the number of university positions available, many of these graduates will need to find employment in industry and government.

Salaries

So, how much can you expect to earn if you pursue one of these challenging scientific careers? Keep reading to learn more about the income outlook in computer science and mathematics.

Computer Professionals

According to the National Association of Colleges and Employers, starting offers for graduates with a doctoral degree in computer science averaged $93,050 in 2005. Starting offers averaged $50,820 for graduates with a bachelor's degree in computer science; $46,189 for those with a degree in computer systems analysis; $44,417 for those with a degree in management information systems; and $44,775 for those with a degree in information sciences and systems.

According to Robert Half International, a firm providing specialized staffing services, starting salaries in 2005 ranged from $67,750 to $95,500 for database administrators. Salaries for networking and Internet-related occupations ranged from $47,000 to $68,500 for LAN administrators and from $51,750 to $74,520 for Web developers. Starting salaries for information security professionals ranged from $63,750 to $93,000 in 2005.

Median annual earnings of computer and information scientists in research were $85,190 in May 2004. Most earned between $64,860 and $108,440; the lowest 10 percent earned less than $48,930; the highest 10 percent earned more than $132,700. Median annual earnings of computer and information scientists in computer systems design and related services were $85,530.

Median annual earnings of database administrators were $60,650 in May 2004. The majority earned between $44,490 and $81,140. Ten percent earned less than $33,380, and 10 percent earned more than $97,450.

Database administrators employed in computer systems design and related services had median earnings of $70,530. For those in management of companies and enterprises, earnings were $65,990.

Network systems and data communication analysts had median annual earnings of $60,600 in May 2004, with most earning between $46,480 and $78,060. The lowest 10 percent earned less than $36,260, and the highest 10 percent earned more than $95,040. Median annual earnings in the industries employing the largest numbers of network systems and data communications analysts are shown below:

Wired telecommunications carriers	$65,130
Insurance carriers	$64,660
Management of companies and enterprises	$64,170
Computer systems design and related services	$63,910
Local government	$52,300

Median annual earnings of all other computer specialists were $59,480 in May 2004; for all other computer specialists employed in computer systems design and related services, earnings were $57,430; those in management of companies and enterprises earned $68,590.

Mathematicians

Median annual earnings of mathematicians were $81,240 in May 2004. Most earned between $60,050 and $101,360. The lowest 10 percent had earnings of less than $43,160, while the highest 10 percent earned over $120,900.

In early 2005, the average annual salary for mathematicians employed by the federal government in supervisory, nonsupervisory, and managerial positions was $88,194; that for mathematical statisticians was $91,446; and for cryptanalysts the average was $70,774.

Parade of Professionals

Now that you know the training you need and the prospects of finding a job, read the following accounts to see what the work of computer professionals and mathematicians is really like.

Steven Brent Assa, Ph.D., Mathematical Research Scientist

Dr. Steven Assa is a research scientist who earned his B.A. in mathematics and Scandinavian literature and his Ph.D. in mathematics from Ohio State University.

Dr. Assa has wanted to be a scientist since childhood, although he initially thought he would pursue a career in psychiatry. Once in college, he realized that what he really liked was mathematics and Scandinavian literature. He says, "Mathematics appealed to me because I thought that God spoke to people through universal laws conveyed in goodness and love, through mathematical equations. Understanding these equations was the same as understanding the way the world is, which is a first step to accepting the beings in the world."

His job is to build a 3-D geometry modeling system for geological applications. He works with geologists, physicists, computer scientists, and other mathematicians, and he says that there are never enough hours in the day for him to talk to all the people that he interacts with. He spends about eight hours at his office and many additional hours thinking about the meaning and elegance of the equations that he manipulates.

"My current job is the most wonderful job that I can imagine," Dr. Assa says. "I may sound over the top on this, but over the past five years I have begun to see the beauty of mathematics in the physics applications that I work on at a level that makes me honored to think that I understand even a small part of their beauty and organic purpose."

A typical day begins with answering mail and checking in with a junior colleague with whom he works very closely, reviewing any questions that either one has about the previous day's collaboration. They decide what aspect of the project to consider and who will look at which issues, then separate for a few hours. Steven makes notes, decides how to approach his projects, and then immerses himself in his work. Although interruptions break his concentration, he says that part of the fun of the job is receiving new issues from users of the computer system that he's built.

Although he finds the work very pleasant, Dr. Assa does get tired from the heavy mental exertion of this job. When this happens, he refers to one of his "classical" mathematical physics books, to gain a sense of clarity and to give himself a chance to avoid his immediate problems for a few minutes.

Dr. Assa describes his job as one that permits him to be a permanent graduate student research assistant, with himself as the boss. What he likes most is being able to propose the majority of his work. Although he works on projects that have a visible payoff for the company, he is able to focus on the parts that he finds exciting. He feels that he is trusted and respected by management, but he has no managerial aspirations himself, preferring to work strictly with mathematics.

What Dr. Assa finds least agreeable about his job is making certain that he is not drafted back into the day-to-day engineering ranks of the company. He worked that way for about nine years and found it to be good training in general computer systems design, product completion, and group effort. Today, however, he prefers having the time to dream. After his first patent was issued, the company realized that his talents could be used more efficiently in his present position.

When asked what advice he'd give to aspiring mathematicians, Dr. Assa says, "I recommend that you never lose your need to understand why things are the way they are. Talk to other people about your ideas and spend your time trying to make something useful out of these ideas. Read, read, read—especially the classics. Clarity of thought is timeless and independent of the problem addressed."

Brian Killen, Software Engineer

Brian Killen is a software engineer who earned his B.S. in computer science from Kansas State University.

Brian became interested in computers while in high school, and during college he served in an internship with a computer services organization. He has also attended numerous seminars on any topic to do with software engineering and development. His main interest has always been to develop products that help people communicate with each other.

Workdays are influenced by whatever is the current project. Projects run in one- to two-year cycles. The beginning of a project involves thinking, designing, and talking to customers; the latter half is spent at the keyboard writing code. The last five months of a project are the busiest and most stressful.

Brian describes the work atmosphere as extremely casual. Although the scheduled office hours are Monday through Friday from 8:30 A.M. until 5 P.M., he usually works fifty to sixty hours per week. During crunch time, it can be seventy hours per week, and the job is very intense. The staff convenes weekly meetings via teleconference with colleagues working on the projects in California and India.

What Brian likes best about his job is creating products for people. What he likes least is the turnaround time for a product, because it takes two years to see results and to feel the full gratification of the job.

Brian recommends that in order to serve in this position effectively, you'll need experience in designing user interfaces, software engineering, and programming—networking, protocol development, and C++ language. You'll also need patience, the ability to work as part of a team, the ability to keep the customer in mind, the skills to work well with a diverse group of people, good communication and interpersonal habits, attention to detail, stamina to work on a project for years, persistence, and insight into where the industry is going.

"You really have to like this kind of work to do this job because it's quite demanding," Brian says. "Long, difficult, stressful hours are fairly common. I'd advise others to obtain as much experience as early as possible because this isn't a job you are really able to understand in college. It's a job you learn by doing. Once you experience the doing, you'll be able to determine if this is something that you truly want to make your life's work."

Celeste M. Combs, Biomechanical Research Engineer

Celeste Combs is a human factors engineer for Microsoft. She earned her bachelor of arts degree in health education and kinesiology from the University of North Iowa, Cedar Falls, and attended the master of science program at the University of Oregon in Eugene (biomechanics) and the master of science program at the University of Washington in Seattle (bioengineering).

Celeste was attracted to her profession because she was focused on improving the lives of others and had a long-standing fascination with human movement and performance. Biomechanics is science that applies physiology and mechanics to understanding movement, which limits injury and helps to improve performance. Her personal philosophy is that human beings interact within larger systems that not only encompass the physical realm but cognitive and emotional areas. In her position at Microsoft, she feels fortunate to work within interdisciplinary teams to reach this larger goal of optimizing the systems within which we live and spend our time daily.

Celeste's career has been influenced by all of her work experiences, including interacting with colleagues. After college, she worked in a business environment, where she gained some applicable business skills that translate to any profession. She changed paths and decided to pursue physiology, gaining the valuable foundation needed for her current environment and graduate work. For five years before attending graduate school, she worked for three employers—as a physical therapy assistant, as a research assistant at the Institute for Aerobics Research in Dallas, and as a research assistant in the research division of a pharmaceutical firm conducting and managing research projects around the country. Each environment was beneficial, giving her experience as well as the opportunity to interact with outstanding scientists and researchers and ultimately providing her with the edge and insight required to do outstanding research and design work at Microsoft, with an emphasis in human factors engineering.

On a daily basis, Celeste conducts biomechanical and design-related research to improve hardware products, such as the mouse, keyboard, and gaming products, in order to optimize them on both a physical and mechanical basis. She interacts with industrial designers, ergonomists, software engineers, mechanical and electrical engineers, and program managers. Each product brings different challenges, and the position requires good communication and writing skills.

"Like many jobs, there are deadlines, decisions, and generally very busy days," Celeste says. "Within that context, I enjoy my job tremendously. I believe that in order to work in these environments, one must enjoy what he or she does and be able to see a broader picture. When I see a product in someone's hand or hear some positive feedback, I feel richly rewarded.

"I would advise potential scientific types to get some experience so that you are sure that this is the profession for you. That's your first challenge. Once this has been established, I would stress that you have an open mind to alternatives. Remember that out of every rejection or negative situation, there are many alternatives and positive situations. So it helps to be flexible. Education and knowledge are always a part of a process. You must realize that success won't come at once, but slowly through experience and time. But you should always seek the courage to live your passion—whatever inspires and motivates you most."

Tom Teska, Computer Consultant

Tom Teska has worked as a computer consultant for over twenty-five years and has been a Certified Network Engineer since 1991.

He earned a B.S. in computer science from the University of Wisconsin in Madison, received training on Netware 4.x administration and design, and took a class on teaching Novell courses.

His father opened a ComputerLand store in 1980, and Tom discovered that he loved working on computers and making them do things that no one else could do. From there, he began helping people use them better. His consulting work lets him help people and work on computers, which he feels is the best of both worlds.

Tom says that his job has changed many times over the years. When he worked in the commercial sector, he operated at a very fast pace. In his work with ComputerLand and Entre stores, he supported upwards of a thousand companies with tens of thousands of employees and typically worked sixty to eighty hours a week for months at a time.

What Tom enjoys most about working as a consultant and support person is being able to get people's PCs to do things that they cannot. Clients call him when they've got a problem that they haven't been able to solve, and he fixes it. It makes him feel good to help people, and he enjoys the thanks he gets from the users in these situations. He also looks forward to the actual work with the computers and has fun while he's working.

Tom is presently employed by a long-term contract consulting firm, where the pace is steady but not overwhelming. He reports to only one client supporting fewer than ten thousand people and now works a standard forty-hour week. When he was assigned to commercial stores, there was no such thing as a typical day, which was one of the things he liked about the work—one day he'd be working with bankers, and the next day he'd be helping teachers in an elementary school. Now that he supports only one company, he does have typical days. He works in a cubicle with several other support people, who install and support applications and maintain the large WAN that is housed here. He also works on the second-level help desk, which means that he gets the problem calls that the first-level people can't solve.

Working in the commercial part of the field gave Tom the opportunity to work with cutting-edge technology. He enjoyed working on new systems that no one had tried before and found it particularly pleasurable to learn new things.

His least favorite aspect of the business is having to solve the same problems over and over. Also, he occasionally has a customer who isn't satisfied, although fortunately this doesn't happen very often.

"I feel that the most important thing about being a consultant is to keep learning," Tom says. "I think it's my job to know more about PCs, networks, and software than my customers. Thus, I constantly seek out new information through reading and taking classes in order to be aware of the new strategies and technologies that come to light virtually every day in this ever-changing field."

Tim Lee, Network Consultant/LAN Administrator

Tim Lee is a network consultant/LAN administrator for Anderson Consulting in Lincoln, Nebraska. He earned a B.S. degree in economics from Kansas State University in Manhattan, Kansas, and an M.B.A. from Kansas State University in Kansas City, Missouri.

Tim acquired the knowledge of computer systems that led to his present job while working in mutual fund processing. He spends about half of his time in day-to-day operations management, implementing changes to the system and finding solutions to ongoing problems. About 30 percent of the day he talks on the phone with clients, helping them solve their computer problems. The other 20 percent is spent documenting what he's done that day to help clients.

Work is performed at the client's site, so the setting depends on the client's work atmosphere. The most hectic times are when the computer goes down or when new programs are being implemented. Tim works an average of forty to fifty hours per week, including some evenings.

Tim most enjoys having the freedom to do what is best for the client. He appreciates that the company's management encourages staff to be creative with their ideas. The consultants work in a team setting, which Tim enjoys. He likes his boss's hands-off management style and feels trusted to do what is best for the client. What he dislikes is working under the constraints of a state budget, because funds are limited. On the positive side, however, it presents challenges in offering the customer the most for the money that is available.

"In order to serve in this position, you need to have good problem-solving skills, PC and network experience, experience in customer service and relationship building, organizational skills, networking skills, and the ability to work in a team setting," Tim recommends. "I'd advise prospective candidates to learn as much as you can about computer software and systems. It's important to develop great problem-solving and customer-relations skills. You have to be a people person. Gain experience as you study. Always keep in mind that your experience will help you in the future."

For More Information

Additional information about computer careers is available from the following associations:

Association for Computing Machinery (ACM)
2 Penn Plaza, Suite 701
New York, NY 10121
www.acm.org

Association for Information Systems
PO Box 2712
Atlanta, GA 30301
www.aisnet.org

Association for Women in Computing
41 Sutter Street, Suite 1006
San Francisco, California 94104
www.awc-hq.org

Canadian Information Processing Society
CIPS National
2800 Skymark Avenue, Suite 402
Mississauga, ON L4W 5A6
Canada
www.cips.ca

IEEE Computer Society
1730 Massachusetts Avenue NW
Washington, DC 20036
www.computer.org

Information about the designation Certified Computing Professional is available from:

Institute for Certification of Computing Professionals (ICCP)
2350 East Devon Avenue, Suite 115
Des Plaines, IL 60018
www.iccp.org

Information about the designation Certified Quality Analyst is available from:

Quality Assurance Institute
2101 Park Center Drive, Suite 200
Orlando, FL 32835
www.qaiworldwide.org

For more information about the field of mathematics, including career opportunities and professional training, contact:

American Mathematical Society
201 Charles Street
Providence, RI 02904
www.ams.org

Canadian Mathematical Society
577 King Edward, Suite 109
Ottawa, ON K1N 6N5
Canada
www.cms.math.ca

Mathematical Association of America
1529 Eighteenth Street NW
Washington, DC 20036
www.maa.org

For a resource guide on careers in mathematical sciences, contact:

Conference Board of the Mathematical Sciences
1529 Eighteenth Street NW
Washington, DC 20036
www.cbmsweb.org

For specific information on careers in applied mathematics, contact:

Society for Industrial and Applied Mathematics
3600 University City Science Center
Philadelphia, PA 19104
www.siam.org

Information on obtaining a mathematician or computer science position with the federal government may be obtained from the Office of Personnel Management. Visit the official website at www.usajobs.com.

In Canada, visit www.jobs-emplois.gc.ca for information on federal jobs.

About the Author

Jan Goldberg's love for the printed page began well before her second birthday. Regular visits to the bookbindery where her grandfather worked produced a magic combination of sights and smells that she carries with her to this day.

Childhood was filled with composing poems and stories, reading books, and playing library. Elementary and high school included an assortment of contributions to school newspapers. While a full-time college student, Goldberg wrote extensively as part of her job responsibilities in the College of Business Administration at Roosevelt University in Chicago. After receiving a degree in elementary education, she was able to extend her love of reading and writing to her students.

Goldberg has written extensively in the occupations area for *Career World* magazine for high school and middle school students, as well as for the many career publications produced by Cass Communications. She has also contributed to a number of projects for educational publishers, including Capstone Publishing, Publications International, Scott Foresman, Addison-Wesley, and Camp Fire Boys and Girls. She is coauthor of the revised and updated edition of *Perfectionism: What's Bad About Being Too Good?*

As a feature writer, Goldberg's work has appeared in *Parenting Magazine, Today's Chicago Woman, Opportunity Magazine, Correspondent, Chicago Parent, Successful Student, Complete Woman,*

North Shore Magazine, and the Pioneer Press newspapers. In all, she has published more than 350 pieces as a full-time freelance writer.

In addition to *Careers for Scientific Types and Others with Inquiring Minds*, she is the author of more than a dozen books published by McGraw-Hill.